ALL SAINTS' CHURCH, F
THE STORY OF A WARWICKSHIRE

JOHN STRINGER
FOR NEVILLE ELLIS

NOVEMBER, 2012

All Saints
HARBURY

Typeset in Minion Pro 11/13.5 pt
Printed by Impress Print, Corby, Northamptonshire

All profits from the sale of this book are solely for the use of the Parochial Church Council of All Saints' Church, Harbury.

ISBN Number 978-0-95509-914-4

ᵔ Acknowledgements ᵔ

MANY THANKS TO:

Celia Barrett, Jeff Bedford, Maurice Bristow, Nigel Chapman, Beryl Checkley, Isobel Clarke, Neville Ellis, Dr Sarah Foot, Joanna Friel, The Reverend Craig Groocock, Drs Sharon and John Hancock, Felicity Harris, Tony 'Bunny' Hodges, William Jones, Anne and John Moore, Dr Anne Polden, Professor Patrick Polden, David Steele, Ken Stephenson, Sally Stringer, Ralph Swadling, Susan Tall, Tony Thomas and The Staff of the Warwickshire County Records Office.

I am greatly indebted to Mike Abbott for his design, typography and photographic skills which have hugely enhanced my text.

PHOTOGRAPHIC CREDITS

I am grateful to the Warwickshire County Record Office and its website *Windows on Warwickshire* for permission to publish images used in this book on pages 8, 53, 56, 75 and 79.

David Armstrong: p100, Craig Groocock and family
William Jones: p34, Harbury bell in action
Roger Mortimer: Colour plate, Richard Jago
Additional photography by Mike Abbott

David Steele has kindly given permission to publish his stunning contemporary photographs of the church, including those on the front and back covers.

∼ Introduction ∼

*And there are also many other things which Jesus did, the which,
if they should be written every one, I suppose that even the world
itself could not contain the books that should be written.*
St John's Gospel, chapter 21, verse 25, King James Version.

THIS IS THE STORY of a church and of a Church. I am no historian, and this is not a history. It the story of a building, and of a worshipping Christian community that can trace its line back, unbroken, for well over a thousand years.

There has been a stone church in the village of Harbury for seven hundred years. Even if there had been as few as five services a week, there have been over three hundred thousand celebrations in the building. The true figure might be nearer half a million. If we estimate about a hundred new worshippers each century, that's around a hundred thousand different people through its door over the years. Fifty-eight named ministers have served the parish to date; and possibly as many curates.

All that is to say that this small book cannot possibly tell the whole story of All Saints, Harbury. There will be people and events that are not recorded here. There isn't room.

WHAT'S MISSED OUT

There are at least three other books that remain to be written: one is the story of the two Wesleyan chapels in the village which were also centres of Christian worship up to the 1930s. I've touched on a period from their history. Another is a recent history of All Saints, recording the changes and developments, the use of the church as a theatre and a concert hall, and the numerous groups and organisations that have grown up around it. A third is a new history of the village. The Internet has arrived since the fine village history *Hungry Harbury* was written and a wealth of information is now available, literally at your fingertips.

I've had a huge amount of help from so many people in putting this book together. I believe I have named them all in the credits. But I want to make special mention of Neville Ellis, farmer, craftsman, bellringer and local amateur historian. He is responsible for the original research that led to my putting this story together. Ill health prevented him completing the book, but he has guided me at every stage.

Because of Neville, I had a picture that I've carried in my mind throughout the writing of this book. It's of an early morning, around seven hundred and forty years ago. A group of men are standing shivering on a patch of dewy grass. One of them carries pegs and rough string. He starts to hammer the pegs into the ground, marking out a rough rectangle. 'Right, lads', he says. 'We're building here'.

CONVENTIONS

This is a story, not a history. There are no *footnotes* and no *references*. As far as I could, I've used two sources for each statement; but I cannot promise complete accuracy. I've not introduced inaccuracies, but I've not let historical precision get in the way of a good tale.

The tale is told chronologically. When something is first mentioned, *I've told its whole story*. For example, the first historical record of the church bells is in 1522, so from the sixteenth century I've traced the history of the bells through to the present day in one piece.

The lives of our ministers are interspersed with the events that took place during their periods in office. That way, you can link the character and the event: the extraordinary William Wight with the National School, and the courageous Matthew Hole with the Victorian rebuild.

I've used the lower case word '*church*' to describe the building; the capitalised word '*Church*' to describe the worshipping community. I've used the word '*lay*' in its formal sense of anybody other than a church minister, and '*congregation*' for churchgoers.

All Saints is a church in the Southam *Deanery* of the Coventry *Diocese*. But it has wandered a bit. It was for a period in the Worcester Diocese – and in the Diocese of Coventry and Lichfield.

VICAR OR RECTOR?

All Saints has sometimes had a *vicar*, and sometimes a *rector*. The explanation for this is complicated. Historically, all parish priests were responsible for the 'cure of souls'. Parish priests in the Church of England were divided into rectors, vicars, and perpetual curates. The parish clergy and church were supported by tithes; like a local tax (traditionally of ten percent) levied on the personal as well as agricultural output of the parish. A rector directly received both the greater and lesser tithes of his parish while a vicar received only the lesser tithes (the greater tithes going to the lay holder of the living). A perpetual curate with a small parish, and often aged or infirm, received neither greater nor lesser tithes, but only a small salary (paid sometimes by the diocese).

Quite commonly, parishes that had a rector as priest also had glebe lands attached to the parish. The rector was then responsible for the repair of the chancel of his church – the part dedicated to the sacred offices – while the rest of the building was the responsibility of the parish. Today, the roles of a rector and a vicar are essentially the same. Which of the two titles is held by the parish priest is historic. Some parishes have a rector, others a vicar, and the term rector has also been re-introduced to designate the priest in charge of a team ministry.

VICARAGE OR RECTORY?

One result, of course, is that some of our ministers have lived in the *vicarage*, and some in the *rectory*, though fortunately, the road has always been Vicarage Lane. Before the building of the last vicarage though, it seems that our ministers still lived in Church Street...

The Bishop can 'suspend a benefice', appointing a *priest-in-charge*, who simply holds a licence rather than freehold. The appointment of priests in charge rather than incumbents is sometimes done when parish reorganisation is taking place or to give the bishop greater control over the deployment of clergy. Our current minister, Craig Groocock, was appointed as a priest-in-charge.

We currently have a curate, too – Annie Goldthorp. A *curate* is a person who is invested with the care or cure of souls of a parish. In English-speaking countries, a curate is an assistant to the parish priest. Her duties and offices are called a curacy. Annie was recently ordained a priest – of which, more later.

Finally, our last minister, Roy Brown, was appointed *canon*. A canon (from the Latin canonicus, meaning 'relating to a rule') is a priest or minister who is a member of certain bodies of the Christian clergy and subject to an ecclesiastical rule or canon.

Do enjoy your read. For a village where not much appears to have happened, Harbury has an amazing history.

John Stringer, November 2012

The interior of All Saints' church, early 1900's

ᖇ 1066 and all that ᖇ

THE PARISH OF HARBURY is bounded on the east by the river
Itchen and on the west by the Fosse Way. At Deppers Bridge over
the river Itchen, the ground is only 260 feet (80 metres) above sea
level, but the ground climbs from there, as cyclists into the village will
tell you, to 400 feet (120 metres). There is a benchmark confirming this
on the wall of the church. The benchmark is on a projecting pier in the
centre of the south wall, slightly above the top of the rainwater channel.
The OS map shows the benchmark on the buttress at the south end of
the tower. The map is unlikely to be correct, as the benchmark would
have been placed at the same time as the church extension was built.
The timing fits with the growth of the Ordnance Survey. The map shows
the benchmark as being slightly under eight feet above the corner of
Church Street. (All this is irrelevant today as GPS satellites offer much
greater precision!)

But, satellites or not, Harbury is on a hill and so more easily defended,
and this, and the abundance of fresh water, must have made it an attractive site for a settlement in prehistoric times. The village was named
Herberbury (hence Heber Drive) or Erburga after its Iron Age Queen
Heber and her *byrig* – her camp or bury. (Accurate spelling was not
essential in those days, and you will come across other versions, including Hereburgebyrig in the year 1002, Erburgeberie in 1200, Erburberie
and Elberberie.) One book assures us that the name comes from *erle*
or principal, with *byrig* or town. But it's wrong on everything else, too.

A 'bury' indicates a manmade mound or earthwork, and traces of
this can be seen in the lane behind the houses on Hall Lane. Part of the
bury is in the gardens of Harbury House.

THE CUTTING

The Victorian railway cutting, a mile and a half long and 110 feet deep (in
old money!) at its deepest point, carved through this hill on the former
Great Western Railway line to Birmingham, changed the character of the
village in two ways. First, it introduced huge numbers of navigationals

or 'navvies' – manual labourers with a powerful thirst – to the village, which explains our large number of public houses. Second, it drained away water from many of the wells, making the land less productive. Hence, possibly, the village nickname of 'Hungry Harbury'. But the village still grew – from 121 souls in 1086, to 480 in 1665, 662 in 1730, 857 in 1801 and 1039 in 1841.

In Saxon times there was a track through the village, but there was never a main road, so that in 1625 the village was described as 'no thoroughfare'. The absence of a main road and so of through traffic make living here attractive to this day.

"View of Harbury from the great railway cutting"
The village in Victorian times. The windmill has its sails.
From a publication by William Wight, minister from 1852-1865

THE FIRST CHURCH

We don't know when Christianity first came to the village. There has been a Christian priest in Harbury since at least the time of the Domesday

Book in 1086. But we cannot be sure that there was a church building, and he may have been based in the Manor House. Ownership of a 'manorial church' was grounds for promotion for a nobleman (from Eorl to Thegn, no less). So we can guess that Harbury's major landowner would have had a priest. That doesn't preclude a village church as well – and indeed there was squabbling in some areas between manor house and minister and village church about who collected tithes and other income.

Saint Bede, the Northumbrian monk, had called for a village-based ministry early in the eighth century. By the tenth century, a priest in every village was assumed.

It was common in the Middle Ages for the people of the church to meet in houses and homes, much as some groups do today. But if there were a church building before the present one, it seems reasonable to suppose that it was on or close to the present site, and that it was a wood and thatch structure. It would have been 'cellular': a two-box structure with a nave and chancel. No trace of it remains.

There was a tradition of building Christian churches on pagan sites of worship, aiming to literally bury them. Indeed, many church sites were on pagan springs, which were a handy source of water for baptism. So it is possible that All Saints was built on just such a spring; or at least, a pagan site. In some areas, this backfired a bit, as Christians were reluctant to attend a pagan site, seeing the churches as tainted by association.

A village church was entitled to collect tithes. Harbury church would have collected a plough-scot, too – a penny for every plough team – and a soul-scot or 'corpse-present' – money for each burial.

The Churchyard

The churchyard is raised, of course. You approach the main, south door of the church along a shallow valley between the raised ground of the graveyard. Early graves would have been quite shallow. There was no tradition of burying valuables with the dead (though there was one period when shrouds had to be made of local wool, to boost the wool trade), so there was no grave-robbing. The height might have been due to the burying of bodies, one on top of the other.

But the height may be due to the soil added to the site later during a cholera epidemic, when the bodies of the victims were buried deeply to prevent infection. In 1848 there were a number of Acts of Parliament ordering that bodies be buried deeper, and it is likely that the churchyard was raised then, probably using spoil – waste material – from the quarry.

It is suggested that this may also have discouraged grave-robbers (or 'Resurrection Men') seeking corpses for medical training (although they would be unlikely in rural areas). Some of the Harbury graves are under 'ledgers' – hefty slabs of stone that made stealing the body a challenge. The first gravestones actually made of stone were erected in the sixteenth century. There are very few with a date pre-1700. Further burials in the churchyard have been prohibited from April, 1915.

While Antony Rowe was minister, a dead tree in the middle of the churchyard was replaced with a Tree of Heaven on Maurice Bristow's advice.

Maybe under the churchyard – a long way under – there are Saxon burials. And just possibly, a timber structure was built here that was Harbury's first separate church building. Timber churches were common in Saxon times. They were replaced by stone buildings as stone became popular for houses. After all, if houses are built of stone, why not the House of the Lord?

A full list of the names on the churchyard tombstones is available on the Birmingham and Midland Society for Genealogy and Heraldry website, fiche number I137. Many are familiar; the Cs including Capps, Ceney and Cleaver, for example.

❧ 1150 A new church ❧ and a quarrel

THE EARLY HISTORY of All Saints is complicated. It all began with a fight – probably over land and money. There had been an argument between the canons of Kenilworth Priory and Geoffrey de Clinton around the middle of the 12th century about the rights to land. Finally, the church of All Saints Harbury was granted to the priory together with a virgate – about a quarter of an acre. A further virgate was added 'in remorse for having laid violent hands on the canons in a quarrel as to their rights to it'. Rows like this were not uncommon. A church was a source of income, and so of strife.

The gift was ratified by Robert de Lodbroke and his brother William, a priest, and by Robert's son Ralph de Megre. The witnesses to the gift were Robert's wife, her mother and her uncle, the exotically named Ralph de Parco. The land was appropriated to the priory by Bishop Muschamp in the reign of King John, 1166-1216. Patronage remained with the convent. Just before the Dissolution of the Monasteries (between 1536 and 1541) they granted a 'turn' (access to the land) which was not exercised until 1550, to Nicholas Cooke and others. The rectory and 'advowson' were retained by the crown until 1589-90, when they were granted to Richard Thekeston 'and others'.

An advowson is a form of property which may he bought, sold or given away and is subject to civil law - a kind of lend-lease arrangement: 'the right of nomination or presentation to an ecclesiastical benefice' – of choosing and appointing a priest. An advowson is held by the patron of a church, who presents a ministry candidate to the appropriate Bishop for institution and induction. The Bishop may refuse the nomination.

In 1291 the church had a value of £12. 4s. 8d. In 1535 the vicarage was worth £5. In 1736, land in Harbury was given for repair and maintenance of the church, together with relief of the poor. The land was sold and the proceeds of the sale invested, bringing in an annual income of £47 4s. 8d. This is the origin of the John Jorge charity, and its income was used for the tower and spire, but not the chancel – because that part of the church was the responsibility of the priest. It also funded bedding and clothing for the 'deserving poor' resident in the parish. It still meets to this day, though there is less call on it for mattresses. This is the only written evidence that the church ever had a steeple. But support for a steeple would go some way to explaining why the tower is so massively buttressed.

❧ 1200 or thereabouts ❧
Why build a church?

THE COUNTRYSIDE in the Middle Ages would have looked very different to today, with large fields held and farmed in common. Our present landscape, with its fields, villages and towns, was established much later, following the Acts of Enclosure in the 1700s and 1800s. But far from being a period of ignorance the Middle Ages was a time when crafts and skills, from clock-making to the construction of mills, flourished. And it was a time when many village churches – like All Saints, Harbury – were built.

The purpose of a church building is not in doubt: a church is a centre of the Christian faith. It was faith that led to the building of All Saints. In the Middle Ages, the Church held a monopoly on faith; the Church was both rich and powerful. To the people of the Middle Ages, this exalted position was to be shown off, and building was one effective way of displaying power and wealth. So churches were endowed to parade the wealth of their patrons. This led to competition in church building - in size, style and craftsmanship. One way of estimating the importance of the church's patron is to look at the cost of the work; because it was the patrons of the churches who paid for each building.

Most patrons were senior churchmen, but lords and even kings patronised church building for a mixture of motives, including pride and prestige. Many were moved to build through faith and piety, their actions inspired by deep religious principles. The Middle Ages was the time of vows; and sometimes, churches were erected in fulfilment of a vow. Medieval priests, under a vow of celibacy, had no legitimate children and so founded no dynasty, and may have chosen to leave a building as a legacy of their lives.

WHERE DID THE MONEY COME FROM?

We don't know how much it cost to erect All Saints in Harbury. Records of church costs were lost during the Reformation. But we do know the cost of replacing Westminster Abbey, built around the same time (1245-72). Around £2100 was spent in each of those 27 years. It's difficult to compare these costs with modern day values, but that's certainly more than a million pounds a year. (That compares favourably with castles, incidentally. Not being so well finished or so decorative, castles were very much cheaper – and quicker – to build.) Some of the money came from the people, of course, much of it from tithes. At the time, the population of England was around six million, or over a million households. A calculation of the building costs of churches in the thirteenth century works out at an annual levy of £500 a household – the rough equivalent of around half present day council tax.

Another source of money was the Church estates: the land belonging to the Church. These produced food, goods and rent. After the clergy had been fed, the huge surplus was sold, and this helped to fund church building. This was to the general good, because it employed so many people. The church paid the wages of an army of craftsmen, labourers and suppliers. Church building was a Christian act to the benefit of the whole economy.

WHY ALL SAINTS?

A new church was often dedicated to a saint, and was a setting for services in their honour. The church would sometimes contain a relic – theoretically some body part – of that particular saint. Relic comes from the same root as 'remains'. and a reliquary often stored the remains of a saint – like St Catherine's head in Siena, and her body in Rome, or the remains of John the Baptist, recently claimed to have been discovered in Bulgaria. (A questionable find; they could be his remains, alleged to be his remains, or just a reliquary alleged to contain his remains. Relics are like that.)

Our church may have been called All Saints because we have no relic of any individual saint. The first of November, All Saints' Day, also called All Hallows and Hallowmass, is the day when the lives of all the saints are celebrated. So on All Saints' Day, the congregation still remembers and gives thanks for the lives of all – not just one – of the saints.

The first millennium celebrations had led to an awakening of religious activity. Many churches were built in the next few hundred years. The most common dedication is to the Virgin Mary. 'All Saints' runs a close second.

∽ 1270 ∽
The first stone church

T HE AUTHORITATIVE GUIDE to Warwickshire's historic build-
ings is Pevsner's *Buildings of England*, and it gives short shrift to Harbury. The church gets a few lines, and these suggest that the nave and chancel were built first, and the tower and south aisle later, although still in the thirteenth century. This makes some sense – you can worship in a church without a tower.

However, Neville Ellis, a local amateur historian, believes the tower was built first, placed alongside the wooden Saxon church. The tower would have been a place of refuge in troublesome times. One piece of evidence for this is that the tower once had its own door, separate from the door of the church. You can see the 'shadow' of it on the south side of the tower. Another is that the tower appears to be built in a different, poorer style than the rest of the church – especially the chancel. The tower is built from rubble – roughly shaped stones, possibly collected from the fields – with only the corners cut to shape. Building would have been a slow process. The builders would have burnt lime and thrown it into water. This basic cement, mixed with sand, would have made the mortar for the tower. Because it was slow to set, the builders could only raise the tower by eighteen inches or so a week.

If this was the case, the tower room might have been accommodation for the owner and builders. There might have been a belfry, and even a treasury. With its narrow windows, small original door and spiral staircase, it would have been hard to attack. The staircase is defensive; it spirals clockwise. A defender standing on an upper step has both height and the freedom to use his right arm. The attacker – unless left-handed – would have the central pillar in his way.

If Neville is right, the tower was built as a defence against the King's armies, who 'laid waste' to the village in the eleventh century, taking all its plough animals and leaving the inhabitants with no means of feeding themselves. (This would be one of several alternative explanation for the nickname 'Hungry Harbury'). An alternative, suggested to me by a Medieval historian, is that its defensive nature dates from the 'Baron's War' of the 1260s.

WAS THERE A SPIRE?

The tower you see on All Saints now bears little resemblance to the one you might have seen in the thirteenth century. That tower may have had a tall spire, like the one our Victorian architect later built at Radway. That would explain the John Jorge bequest to maintain the tower and spire. It's not certain what happened to it.

Maybe it was dismantled, or perhaps, like the spire of Kibworth church, it fell down. In any event, the church tower was later topped by the more modest pyramid seen in the engraving from 1817. But there is a rumour of a falling out between the builder and the patron who was footing the bills. The result was a lash-up that topped the tower for centuries.

The spire of Kibworth church fell on July 23rd, 1825

From the beginning, the structure leaned. The slow collapse of the tower to the west has been halted by massive buttresses, the south buttress later to carry a painted sundial. The buttresses themselves had to be reinforced, and several weathered layers can be seen. The original sundial was built in, which suggests that this buttress was at least added to in the seventeenth century. The third, top stage of the tower, according to Pevsner, was built in Georgian times, and has the brick, in Flemish bond, resembling castle battlements, you see when you look up today. The original medieval church had a nave and chancel,

and just one aisle. The nave is the main body of the church, with a name that reminds us of the navy, of ships and the sea, and if you look upwards at the roof it is as if you are looking into an inverted boat. (Indeed the name comes from the Medieval Latin word for ship, *navis*). A pleasing suggestion is that the nave is a ship in which the congregation is sailing to heaven. The roof you are looking at is not entirely the one built seven hundred years ago, however, but a Victorian renovation using some of the original timbers.

THE CHANCEL

The chancel door

The chancel is the space where the altar stands, from the medieval for 'lattice'. It is the responsibility of the incumbent – the minister. That may be why the John Jorge charity was for the upkeep of the tower only – and not for the bit managed by the vicar. The minister even had his own door – a small door, hidden

The rood screen in the 1940s

these days behind a curtain, on the south side of the chancel. It offered him the opportunity to come and go to services without the need to meet the congregation.

In the chancel, the ministers, and often the choir, were housed, and the original chancel was divided from the nave and its congregation by a rood screen, often a lattice, through which the lay people could see the ministers.

Services would have been in Latin, incomprehensible to many of the congregation. The priest would chant, and the verger would respond for the people. Traditionally, the rood screen supported a rood or crucifix (*rood* is Anglo-Saxon for cross). It kept people and animals out of the chancel. The rood screen was taken out in the twentieth century and converted to a fire surround and overmantle for a North Country rectory.

All Saints' chancel is not in a perfect line with the nave. This was not uncommon in Medieval churches, and had nothing to do with poor architecture. The church building was thought to resemble the body of Christ, with the nave his body and the chancel his head. Illustrations of Christ on the cross show him with his head tilted to the right (or 'good') side, and some church buildings, including ours, reflect this position with a slant to the north. This angle is sometimes given as eleven degrees. One side of the recent wooden chancel dais is longer than the other to square the front off with the church.

THE AISLES

The original church had just one, south, aisle. If you are thinking of the word 'aisle' in its modern meaning of passageway, think again. This aisle is a wing of a church, separated from the main church or nave of All Saints by an arcade of thirteenth century pillars. The south, or right side of the church as you look east, or towards the front, is its medieval aisle. There was a good reason for building an aisle on the south side. The sun crosses the sky on the south side, and so the windows here caught its light and heat.

This, then, was the first stone church. It was traditional that the door into the church should be in the south side – and the present door is on the south – but it may not have been the original entrance. There are breaks in the stonework at the foot of the tower, which suggest that there was a door here – not where the present door is. or possibly, like many churches and cathedrals, it had a door on the west side – at the back – now lost. Neville Ellis believes so.

Outside, in the boundary wall, there is a bricked up doorway. Ordnance Survey (OS) maps show footpaths leading directly to the church from both Harbury Hall and the old Wagstaffe School building. The path from the Hall cuts straight through the boundary wall for the convenience of the residents. However. there is no evidence of the ornate archway that admitted the Peyto family to St Giles church in nearby Chesterton. Almost everything else you see in stone or brick is a later

The altar and reredos in the 1940s.
The four apostles are symbolised: the divine man for Matthew,
the winged lion for Mark, the winged ox for Luke
and the rising eagle for John.
A brass plate reads: The gift of Elizabeth Sabin, Whit Sunday 1879

addition, and there were some significant changes in Victorian times – including the building of a north aisle to match the existing south one.

LOST DECORATIONS

One more thing. The medieval church would have been plastered inside. The stonework would have been invisible to the congregation gathered in the nave and aisle. Traditionally, the plaster would have been covered in paintings depicting scenes from the Bible. (There are some of these surviving in St John the Baptist at Avon Dassett).

One, rather patronising, explanation is that these pictures were for the education of the illiterate. Unable to read books, they learned instead from the illustrations. But that doesn't make sense to me. Surely, if you know the stories, whether you were told them, or were able to read them for yourself, the pictures serve the same purpose? They remind you of your Bible, inspire and uplift you. Without this knowledge, the pictures would be meaningless. In any event, the plasterwork pictures in most churches did not survive the rule of Parliament in the 1640s. These fripperies were stripped from our churches, and with them, the plaster, leaving the bare stone. All this was built, to quote the description that rates All Saints as a Grade 2 listed building, of 'square, coursed, limestone rubble'. There is some sandstone in the chancel, and some ironstone in the chancel, too. Presumably there was an altar – but not the strikingly decorated Victorian reredos we see today.

CHURCH RESOURCES

By 1297, every parish church was expected to be fully equipped. Each church was to have 'a chalice of silver or silver gilt; a ciborium or cup of silver or pewter; a pyx or box of silver or ivory for consecrated bread; a chrismatory for holy oils; a censer or incense boat; and a holy water vessel'.

Fixtures were to include a stone altar and font (locked against theft of consecrated water); images of the Virgin Mary, candlesticks and crosses. Later, prayer books and books of collects (daily prayers) were regularly inspected, along with the rest of the resources. Quality and condition were important!

Many of the beams in the present day roof
are from the first medieval church

ᔍ 1270 or thereabouts ᔍ

BUILDING A MEDIEVAL CHURCH *'needed the whole community... inspired by faith, driven on by pride in their institutions and culminating in their work'.*

Tom McNeill, *Faith, Pride and Works*

One morning, somewhere in the second half of the thirteenth century, a group of men must have gathered on a slight rise in the middle of a village of wooden houses to build the village's first stone church. If Neville is right, this church was patched on to the existing tower.

To their east was the market town of Southam. Looking to the west, they could perhaps see the tower of the Norman church of St Mary's, Warwick.

Running conveniently north/south alongside their chosen site was a trackway from Wappenbury to Radway. This would be a handy road for their building materials. You can still follow the Wappenbury Way today in footpaths and bridle paths, through Ufton, Church Terrace, Ivy Lane and the playing field, and on towards the M40. There is even a motorway bridge for it. Beside it, in the corner of Itchington Holt, is a burial mound or barrow. Building materials to Harbury were brought by ox-cart, although river transport was usually preferred because barges were cheaper and carried more.

Around the site would be stone-cutters' workshops, kilns to burn lime for mortar, forges for metal-workers, store houses and glass kilns. Pits were dug for long saws to cut the beams. These were dragged up and down by workmen standing below and above.

The most important men were the master craftsmen. Experienced, sharp-eyed and strong, they were so important that it is possible in some churches to see from the architecture when one master replaced another. And, course, the master might change his own individual style. A change of style will mean the retraining of his craftsmen, and is not achieved overnight.

THE MASTER MASON

Back to our little huddle of workmen.

The master mason would be eyeing up the site, taking compass bearings for an east window and chancel, a nave and tower. The master mason was pre-eminent, but he could not work without the cooperation of the other trades: the master carpenter, for example. Much of the work of the master carpenter was temporary. His team would build the scaffolding, and probably the cranes to lift the stones and wooden beams. His permanent contribution to All Saints would be the roof and its timbers. Master craftsmen were well respected, rising through society by ability rather than through birth. The master mason and master carpenter of New College, Oxford, dined with the Bishop of Winchester at the foundation of the building, and their servants dined with the college fellows. By contrast, skilled journeymen, paid by the day, without business contacts or capital, made up the unsung but vital subcontractors.

Where did the design of All Saints come from? Mostly from the experience and eye of the master mason. There was no 'Mason's Monthly' to bring him up to date with the latest designs, and no website to turn to for inspiration. But there were conferences for masons, at which ideas were exchanged and building techniques discussed. These attracted masons from many countries. So each mason had his own drawings and cloth rolls containing essential measurements and stress calculations. This was his reference book. He had a very good eye, too. Modern computer modelling of flying buttresses has shown that they are placed on medieval cathedrals exactly in the right place to take the force from an arch, even though the word 'force' was not even in use in those times to describe any physical effect.

The master mason would have his own idea of structure and proportions, and this would stamp his signature on the building. When the first mason of Canterbury cathedral tragically fell and was paralysed, another took his place, and experts can see from the structure where the change in direction took place. The mason of All Saints put his signature on the building in the form of a mason's mark, to the left of the present south door, at about eye level.

CUTTING THE ROCK: PIECE WORK

The master mason would have a good eye for stone, too – its grain and other qualities. Large chunks of stone were freed at the quarry. There is limestone under the village, and sandstone was once quarried at Bishop's Itchington. Holes, drilled in the stone, were left to freeze in the winter. The expanding ice split the rock. Or the rock was heated

The mason's mark on the church

with fires and then suddenly cooled with buckets of water, which had the same effect. (Harbury stone is easy to split when wet. When cut, it is weatherproof, and resistant to frost.)

Then the masons would get to work, drawing chalk lines on the rock. The rock was roughly cut using chisels with rough, serrated edges. Their hand tools were mallets, chisels and drills turned with a bow. Finally, rubbing with other, harder stones smoothed and shaped each stone. This was the original 'piece-work'. The masons would mark their work individually – they would be paid by the piece. They would pre-cut stones, and even whole pillars or columns, in the quarry. This made sense, especially where a row of columns or a course of stones was required, because uniformity of shape could be assured. At least the stone for All Saints did not have to come far. The pillars in the south aisle are the thirteenth century originals, cut from Harbury stone.

These dressed stones were taken to the mason's lodge at the building site. Here there was a drawing floor, covered with chalk or plaster. Using drawings and wooden templates, the master carver made the more complex stones. These might be installed incomplete and finished in place to avoid damage to fragile pieces. It was hard and demanding work, with a wealth of carefully guarded craft secrets.

The Master Carpenter

Similarly, the timbers were cut to size and shape in the forest, which saved carting waste material away. The carters supplied transport to the site and around it. Individual items might have been manhandled round the site, carried between two men in a stretcher. Or maybe the builders of All Saints had begun to employ that great thirteenth century invention, the wheelbarrow.

The master carpenter saw to the tracing of the ribs that would support the roof on a large, whitewashed tracing floor. There were no common measures. The base unit was possibly the rod – the length of the feet of sixteen men. Not for another four hundred years would there be any standard measurement.

Scaffolding was constructed on site, so that heavy components could be brought up in stages. Oil-soaked linen filled the window spaces until the glass was installed.

We don't know if the first glass was stained – but probably not. There might have been small coloured panels to break the monotony. But there would not have been any yellow. The discovery of sulphide of silver to stain glass yellow did not come until years later.

Clerk and craftsmen

Standing slightly apart from our group, maybe, would be the holder of the purse strings. The clerk was the financial manager appointed by the patron of the church. He would be dealing with the craftsmen and subcontractors. They had little input to the overall design, but were responsible for elements of it. Accounts of contemporary churches record payments for porches, arches and windows entirely built by subcontractors. These might be delivered ready-made from a workshop far away.

We don't know, according to *Faith, Pride and Works*, how much input these people had into the master design. Some important details – a carving, a window – would be left to an individual. But, especially if their work was part of a series, they would need to cooperate with the master mason, and through him, with the patron.

The craftsmen on site would have been apprenticed to their trade or craft around the age of 14. An apprentice would need contacts to get the position, and financial support throughout his apprenticeship. Apprentices were often recruited from the families of other craftsmen, and the effort of paying for apprenticeship would be worth it. Medieval accounts show craftsmen paid two or three times as much as a labourer, and being employed for a longer season in the year. Subcontracting meant that a master craftsman would be supervising gangs, requiring skills of planning and man management as well as manual skills.

THE LABOURERS

Waiting on the fringes on that first morning were the unskilled labourers. Their work was seasonal; mortar could not be laid if there was danger of frost. During the winter, the skilled men made and stockpiled cut stone and timber, ready for use in the warm weather, but there was no work for labourers. In June 1253, for example, 426 men were employed in Westminster building the Abbey. This dropped to a hundred in the November. Most of these were labourers: 220 in June, but only 30 in November. In rural areas like Harbury, there would also be an annual dip in numbers for the harvest too, as labourers returned to the fields.

Tom McNeill, author of *Faith, Pride and Works*, estimates that around 250 men would have been employed on an 'average large project' like All Saints. He believes that around sixty such projects would be taking place at any one time in thirteenth century England. With the addition of carters and subcontractors, there were perhaps 18-20,000 men employed at some time during the year on church building throughout the country.

So imagine two hundred or so men actively employed on building our village church. They built its long nave, the body of the church, its south aisle beyond the pillars to your right, the chancel with its altar and east window, and the tower at its west end (unless the building was grafted to an existing tower). There is as yet no north aisle to your left – that will come much later.

Two sets of footing walls were built, one to carry the arcades and the other to support the exterior walls and buttresses. It took a year or two for these foundations to settle. Their accuracy was checked, horizontally with water-filled troughs and vertically with plumb-lines. Then the church itself went up – probably, traditionally, building from east to west. Heavy stones would be lifted aloft using cranes powered by men walking in 'squirrel cages'. Holes were left for scaffolding beams to be inserted.

There would be plumbers for the lead roof and guttering. There would be glaziers, and plasterers for the interior. There would be smiths, responsible for the tools. Each trade would be answerable to its master. Each would have their part to play in the design, as well as the building, of the church. The finished interior was plastered and then richly decorated with paintings of biblical scenes and saints.

Because of the time the building would take to complete, services probably took place in the unfinished church. The chanting of the masses would be accompanied by the tapping of hammers and chisels, the creak of wooden gears, and the sound of feet on the scaffolding high above.

Finally, on top of the tower it's just possible there was a tall spire. This and the tower itself were already giving trouble. From the beginning, the west wall was leaning outwards…

∾ The Fourteenth, Fifteenth ∾ and Sixteenth Centuries

THE PLAGUE or Black Death in the years 1348 and 49 took its toll of priests as well as the rest of the population. While Harbury, being then as now off the main road, escaped the worst of the disease, it was not immune to market forces and rising costs. Many priests died of the plague, and new candidates were in demand. Before the plague, a priest could be hired for four or five marks a year – or two marks with board and lodging. After the plague, wages soared to ten marks a year. Widowers who had lost their wives in the plague found gainful employment in the Church even if they were illiterate. Working conditions were attractive, though a number of these career changers were criticised for dressing extravagantly, neglecting the tonsure or head shaving, and resorting to taverns and brothels.

We have to hope that Harbury's priests in this period were educated men from wealthy families. Richer benefices went to the wealthy – nearby

Ilmington had six rectors in turn, all from the Montford family. Harbury, always being a poor parish, was perhaps not so lucky. Family connections and patronage mattered. Richard Crosseby, Prior of Coventry, made Nicholas Crosseby – presumably a relative – Rector of Ufton, and later of Holy Trinity, Coventry, on a higher salary, with generous study leave. The rising costs of these new ministers led to the first vestry (church council) meetings, and the election of churchwardens. Maintenance and rebuilding became an issue for many churches, and neglect was common.

The Advowson

In 1598, the advowson – the appointment of a priest - passed to the Wagstaffe or Wagstaff family, of Wagstaffe School fame. Henry and Thomas Wagstaffe 'conveyed the advowson' to Richard Wagstaffe, who later became lord of one of the Harbury manors. It was then passed on to others: Richard Wagstaffe 'presented' in 1633 and 1638, and it then came to James Wright, and he or his son (also James) presented in 1670. Dorothy of Warwick presented in 1711. By 1743, the advowson had passed to the Newsham or Newsam family, and they held it for more than a century. The Reverend Clement Newsam, who died around 1852, was both the church's minister and its patron. On his death, the advowson passed to church trustees.

Two ladies – Mrs Edith Kearney in 1900 and Mrs Beardsworth in 1915 - held the advowson before passing it back to the trustees, who hold it to the present day.

The Reformation

Until the Reformation, All Saints would have been a Roman Catholic church. But following Henry VIII's Reformation in England, it would have become Anglican. This possibly followed the actions of Queen Elizabeth I. The Elizabethan religious settlement was Elizabeth's response to the religious divisions created through the reigns of Henry VIII, Edward VI and Mary I. Described as 'The Revolution of 1559', it was set out in two Acts of Parliament. The Act of Supremacy of 1559 re-established the Church of England's independence from Rome, with

Parliament conferring on Elizabeth the title Supreme Governor of the Church of England, while the Act of Uniformity of 1559 set out the form the English church would now take, including the re-establishment of the Book of Common Prayer.

All this would have meant changes to the government and worship in All Saints, Harbury. And for the first time, there was somewhere to sit, other than around the edges where 'the weak shall go to the wall'. Fixed pews became a feature of churches in the fifteenth century.

VICARS OF HARBURY

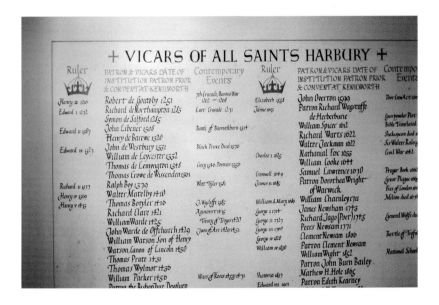

Vicars of Harbury, listed in church by Cecil Bloxham

Two different records exist of the vicars of Harbury – and a variety of spellings. The *Midlands Record* contains names that are not present on the list hanging in church. The great William Wight is missed out altogether, but a 'J White' pops up, mis-spelled and out of order.

Even the invincible internet struggles a bit with references to our church and its ministers over these few hundred years. Searching using

29

their names comes up with some intriguing pieces of information – but given the practice of passing Christian names through families, it's hard to say if these are our priests. So here are a few possibles.

Thomas Botyler (Harbury, 1416) is recorded in 1381 as Prebendary of Bedminster in 1381; by 1367, he is Archdeacon of Northampton, in 1386, Prebendary of Lincoln and 1388, Dean of Windsor. Then he is Bishop of Chrysopolis in 1401, 'Subcollector for the crusade against Bajazet' in 1399 and Suffragan Bishop of Winchester in 1401, and of Worcester in 1420.

These exotic titles – Chrysopolis, Bazajet - arose from the crusader kingdoms. These had the full array of ecclesiastical administration. Like the English royal titles in France, they were presumably kept in being after the loss of these kingdoms. They may have been purely honorary; or there may have been some revenues attached to them.

There is no record of Thomas Prate (1431), but William Watson (1450) was the son of Henry Watson, Canon of Lincoln.

Thomas Wylmot (1456) had a chequered history – if he is the same man. On 21st of March 1411 a writ to the Sheriffs of London ordered them to free *Thomas Wylmot* if 'taken at the suit of Lawrence Markes'. In 1462 he is recorded as Vicar of Ashford, Kent. King Edward granted him another living at Dunton Waylett to help support a chantry college. Later, while chaplain to the vicarage of 'Esshettisford' (Ashford) his duties apparently included the 'keeping of the gaol'.

Richard Wagstaffe de 'Herberburie' was Patron of the living of Harbury in 1599. Robert and Odo are also mentioned – Robert being the last to hold lands.

Peers Newsam (1771) possibly moved to Great Harborough, from where, in 1776, Thomas Peers, apparently his son, entered Rugby School.

This is the thinnest time in our church history, and there is much more to be found out about these and our other ministers for anyone with the skills and patience to research them. A useful database can be found at: **www.theclergydatabase.org.uk/jsp/locations/index.jsp?locKey=2510**

～ 1522 The Bells ～
'the price of one cigarette a day'

THE ENGLISH have always been a bell-ringing nation. A foreign writer at the end of the 16th century said: *'The English… are vastly fond of great noises that fill the ear, such as the firing of cannon, beating of drums, and the ringing of bells. It is common for a number of them that have got a glass in their heads to get up into some belfry and ring the bells for hours together for the sake of exercise.'*

Nothing changes.

CHANGE RINGING

Bells do more than make noise. They summon parishioners to church (once with more success than today) and warn of other, non-church events. In one episode of *Dad's Army* they were rung, wrongly as it turned out, to warn of invasion. They are rung to celebrate events, and to give warning to those not in church that the bread and wine have been raised and consecrated. The peaceful Millet painting *The Angelus* shows two workers in the fields bowed in prayer as a bell rings out from the distant church.

Change ringing is unique to the United Kingdom. It involves ringing the bells in a mathematical pattern, 'tunefully but not melodically'. We know that Harbury has had church bells since the sixteenth century – possibly before. In 1552, it was recorded that 'Harbery' had three bells, a small bell and a handbell. Commissioners from King Edward VI made an inventory of church property throughout the realm. A few years later, these bells would have been rung to celebrate the coronation of the first Queen Elizabeth. The original bells may have been rung from the ground.

There are buttresses in the wall on the north side of the tower to this day, and it may be that they carried the frame of the three ringing bells. By the eighteenth century, two bells had been added, probably cast in Leicester by Watts, or in Chacombe, Northamptonshire, where the Bagley family were master bell founders. In all, the Bagley family cast

440 bells for churches across England. These five bells were recorded on a private survey of 'Herberbury' in 1750.

These first five bells were apparently rung from the ground floor, and there are five holes in the floor of the present ringing chamber for the ropes. Bellringers being active recyclers, the original frame was later used as a lintel at the top of the spiral stairs.

FIVE NEW BELLS

In 1811, the five bells were replaced by new ones made by Mears, the London company, today called the Whitechapel Bell Foundry. These bells shared their makers with the bells of Westminster Abbey, Big Ben and the Liberty Bell. It was around this time that the top of the tower was rebuilt in brick, possibly to receive the new bells, which would have been hung in the rebuilt part of the tower. The bells were engraved with the names of the minister, the Reverend Clement Newsam, and his churchwardens, R Gardener and E Sabin.

Despite their impressive origins, three of the 1811 bells had cracks in their crowns by 1956, when H A Andrews of the Parochial Church Council wrote a foolscap appeal letter to every parishioner.

'CHURCH BELLS ARE THERE FOR ALL THE VILLAGE'

Mr Andrews began his appeal with a reminder of how the bells had been missed when they were silent during the Second World War. The church bells were for everyone in Harbury, he explained, including those who 'attend some other place of worship'. He pointed out that when the bells were ringing, 'about two and a quarter tons of metal is swinging about'.

Since the bell frame was built from timbers reclaimed from before 1811, 'really it should be entirely replaced'. Cracks in the bells had been caused by the rusting and swelling of the iron bolts holding the three largest, and the two smallest would soon follow. The old, worn bearings were a worry, too. 'There is always present the danger that any of these bearings may collapse any time the bells are rung'.

Recasting of the three cracked bells (into four), repairing and retuning the smallest two, new bearings and fittings and a new steel frame would

Casting the new bells for Harbury; Taylor of Loughborough, 1956

come to £1250 (About £6250 in today's money). 'If every man, woman and child in Harbury gave £1 each, the amount would be provided'. An envelope was enclosed, to be returned at a gift service attended by the Archdeacon on February 12th, 1956.

Parishioners were invited to give a small sum weekly. 'If you would all give weekly just the price of one cigarette a day, all the money we need would be in by the time the work has to be paid for'. It's not clear from the letter whether Harbury's toddlers were included in this appeal to donate the price of a gasper, but by 1959, the cracked bells were recast into a new ring of six by Taylor of Loughborough.

A Harbury bell in action, 2006

A RING OF EIGHT

In 1981, to make a total ring of eight, two more bells were taken from the redundant church at Winderton, a hamlet a mile and a half from Brailes in South Warwickshire. These were originally Mears bells, too, like the original bells in Harbury. The Winderton bells were cast by Mears and Stainbank in London in 1877.

The work was completed with donations from the Clarke family, Harry Windsor (the tower captain), Joyce Windsor, and Tom Hauley – of whom more later. Heavy lifting gear, provided for and operated by Andrew Clarke, was used to hoist the bells into place.

On the 5th December, 1981, the bells were dedicated and rung for the first time at a bell ringers' service, attended by the congregation of All Saints and bell ringers from other churches. Ringers are often craftsmen as well as players, and they installed the bells themselves, using part of a bell frame from Christ Church, Spitalfields, which had been replaced with a new one.

The old school bell

Still in the bell tower is a small bell taken from the Wight School and mounted on a wooden frame made by Neville Ellis to instruct new bell ringers in the ancient art. There is also a set of handbells in a cabinet in the tower wall. Originally the property of the Working Men's Club, they were sold to the church on condition that they did not leave the village.

❧ The Seventeenth Century ❧
The Sundial

ON THE SOUTHWEST BUTTRESS of the tower is a sundial carrying a message to prick the conscience: TYME FLYETH. WHAT DOEST THOU? The original dial weathered over time until eventually it was illegible. It was very badly damaged with its surface flaking away. So the present sundial is a replica of the old one. The stone it was set in was kept and is probably in the churchyard.

Harriet James, the restorer, thinks the original was 17th century from the tone of the motto. The more doom-laden ones tend to be from that period! The heavy, block-like style of the lettering is 17th century (from comparison with other sundials - there are thousands recorded by the British Sundial Society). In the early days of clocks, before any form of universal time signal and the electric telegraph, clocks had to be set using a sundial. Perhaps the All Saints' sundial was made to go with the earlier clock. If we knew when the buttress was built that would be a clue as to its date since the dial looks as if it was built in.

Arrival of the restored sundial

READING THE SUNDIAL

The old sundial and its replica were made to face due south. The sundial reads local solar time, which is not the same as clock time. As Harbury is west of the Greenwich meridian, the sun is due south in the village later than at Greenwich. The difference in longitude makes the sundial 5 minutes 49 seconds slower than a sundial at Greenwich. A further difference between clock and sundial time arises because of the tilt of the Earth's axis and variations of speed as it orbits the sun – the so-called 'Equation of Time'.

To read the time on the sundial you look at the shadow of the straight top edge of the gnomon or pointer. To

The original sundial was beyond repair

find Greenwich time from the sundial read the time on the dial, add 5 minutes 49 seconds, add or subtract the value for the equation of time for the date (read from a graph) and in summer add an hour for British Summer Time. Finally, compare the result with the church clock!

RESTORING THE SUNDIAL

Harriet James made a detailed copy of the layout and lettering style and carved it all into a new piece of Portland stone. She expects it to need repainting and gilding every ten years or so. The replica sundial was paid for by Mr and Mrs Clarke of Manor Orchard. It was Mr Clarke's dying mother's wish that the sundial be repaired or replaced.

Finally, the sundial is definitely not a mass dial or mass clock. That is quite a different animal. Mass dials are medieval and are early experiments in dialing before it was fully understood that the gnomon needed to be polar-pointing. There may be some mass dials near the south door of the church (even inside the porch if that was a later addition). They consist of small circles or semi circles with a few lines and/or holes and a central hole.

The sundial is displayed on the restorer's website: **www.harrietjames.sundials.co.uk/restoration.htm**

❧ 1611 ❧
The Wagstaff School

ALYS OR **A**LICE **W**AGSTAFFFE is recorded by a brass in the floor against the west wall. In 1610, Thomas Wagstaffe, a lawyer, purchased land on the north side of the churchyard and erected a limestone school building – the Wagstaffe School. It had a large schoolroom and a two storey west wing for the master, then William Spier, who was on a salary of twenty pounds a year.

In 1611, Thomas Wagstaff or Wagstaffe, or maybe Anne of the same name(s) founded a school in the village. A panel on the wall of the L-shaped building to the north of the church reads:

> *Wagstaff*
> *1611*
> *Estab. by Decree in Chancery*
> *(Butler versus Wagstaffe)*
> *Confirmed by order of ye same court*
> *1637*
> *(Attorn: Gen. versus Baber)*
> *1759*
> *Restored A.D. 1866*

The two-storey west wing probably accommodated the schoolmaster, and the east (with no upper floor) was the schoolroom. In 1949, the *Victoria History* reported that, while the entrance doorway was still there, the original oak door had been removed and was 'lying in the vicarage stables'. The vicarage and its stables are long gone; and so, presumably, is the door.

Wagstaffe's grandson, also Thomas, later sold lands worth more than twenty pounds to secure the schoolmaster and also cover repairs. In 1738, Elizabeth Oughton ended family support for the school, but in 1759, the school was established by court order for 'instructing boys, children of the inhabitants of Harbury, having first learned their letters, in reading, writing and accounts'. The Wagstaffe School continued to serve as the only village school until the arrival of the dynamic Reverend William Wight.

1642 THE PROTESTATION OATH

In July 1641, Parliament passed a bill requiring everyone over the age of 18 to sign *The Protestation*, an oath of allegiance to King Charles I and the Church of England, drawn up on May 3rd of that year. No one could hold a Church or State office without signing.

The aim of the protestation was to avert the looming civil war. The Speaker of the House of Commons sent a letter to the Sheriffs of each county. They and the Justices of the Peace had to sign the protestation. Then, in February or in March 1642, Nathanial Fox, then Minister of All Saints, read the protestation in church to his parishioners and had each one sign, after which the returns were sent to Parliament. Those among the population who could not write marked a cross against their names. Those who did not wish to have their names used in support were also listed in the protestation.

The returns for Harbury are stored in the House of Lords Record Office. Some of the names are still familiar in the village; among them Rich: Wagstaff, Gent.; Tho: Sprawson; John Manne; Tho: Overton; Henry Hawley; and John Sproson – (twice; father and son, perhaps). The courageous John Miles, recorded as owning a forge and so perhaps a farrier or blacksmith, is recorded as 'refused', and Thomas Talbott was apparently excused his signature because his house had burnt down. All this was in vain. King Charles, fearing for his life, had already left London in January, and the English Civil War had begun.

∼ Eighteenth Century ∼ Harbury

BECAUSE HARBURY was some way from any main roads, the Great Plague of 1665 had little effect on the village population. By 1730, there were 148 houses in the village, making it a larger village than average, with seven of these houses uninhabited. But the land around the village was already poor and unproductive, yet another possible explanation of the nickname 'Hungry Harbury'.

Because of these poor farming conditions, Harbury people had become a labour pool for the parishes of Ufton and Chesterton. But the opening of the limestone works resulted in a building boom and a population explosion. Fashionable brick was used for the first time on village houses. There are brick faces on a number of stone-built houses today; a reversal of the present trend for stone facing on brick buildings. By 1841, the population was over a thousand, living in 254 houses – bakers, blacksmiths and butchers among them. There were already five inn-keepers, a tradition the village has maintained to this day. Letters arrived at the Post Office at nine in the morning, and were despatched at six in the evening. In addition, there were weekly carriers to Banbury, Leamington and Warwick. Early in the eighteenth century, a gallery was erected at the West end – the back – of the church, for the choir and musical instruments. Commonly these would be violins, later replaced by an organ. The replacement of the village band by an organ was a common event, recorded in the novels of Thomas Hardy. This gallery was taken down during the Victorian restoration of the church, and the organ put in its present position – still later replaced with the present instrument.

PULPIT AND PEWS

Large pews, shaped like horse-boxes, were put in the nave, with one very large family box pew where the pulpit is now. The eighteenth century pulpit was a 'three-decker' – the lowest deck being the vicar's seat or

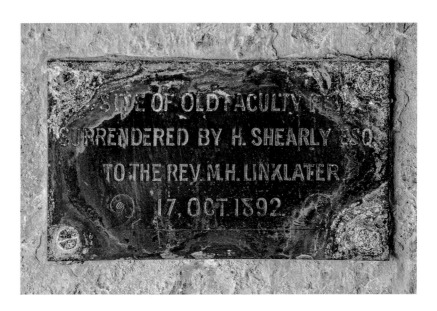

This plaque records the surrender of the front box pew so that the present, octagonal pulpit could be built. It reads: Site of old faculty pew surrendered by H Shearly Esq to Rev M H Linklater 17 Oct 1892

stall. The old medieval font was replaced with the Georgian one now standing in the churchyard, itself later condemned as unworthy for the sacrament of Holy Baptism by the Archdeacon on the grounds that its basin was too small. Pulpits are quite recent innovations (in church terms) becoming popular around the time All Saints was first built.

A common early design was shaped like a wine glass, with the four evangelists – Matthew, Mark, Luke and John – carved on it. Any pulpit would have been made from local wood or stone, simply because of the trouble involved in transporting it. By 1603, pulpits had become compulsory, so that the King's proclamations could be read to the community. Church attendance was compulsory too, with church services easily exceeding an hour. We can imagine an hourglass filled with sand, attached by a bracket to the wall near the pulpit, and the collective sigh of the congregation as the minister turned it over and continued to preach.

Organs are relatively recent innovations, and church music was once made using wind and stringed instruments. The violins were replaced

The old vicarage, facing the church. The curious building to the right might be a chapel, or the parish office.

Another view of the old vicarage, from the corner of Church Street and Vicarage Lane, shown here early in the twentieth century.

by an organ in 1848. The galleries were taken down when the church was rebuilt, and the organ moved to the front, later to be replaced by the present instrument.

THE VICARAGE

It was recorded that the vicarage was 'a neat residence, pleasantly situate near the church'. This was presumably 25, Church Street, opposite the church, which remained the vicarage until the modern building was built on its stabling and yard facing Vicarage Lane.

∿ 1745-1771 ∿
Richard Jago, Poet

IN 1745, Richard Jago became vicar of Harbury. He is widely described as a 'minor' poet, which seems dismissive; but maybe this was because his work did not compare with the greats of his age, or perhaps he was not as widely read. He was, by all accounts, a man who made and kept friends and patrons; and they must have been a particular blessing when tragedy struck his family, then living in the village, in 1751. Jago may have been labelled 'minor', but he has found a place in Dr Johnson's *Works of the English Poets*, as one of the 'additional lives' recorded by Alexander Chalmers. Here, there is a brief biography of the man who was vicar of Harbury (though not always a resident) for 25 years. He was born the third son of the Reverend Richard Jago, rector of Beaudesert, Warwickshire, on October 1st, 1715. He received an 'excellent' classical education at Solihull School, although he did not recall it with enthusiasm:

Hail, Solihull! Respectfully I salute
Thy walls: more awful once, when, from the sweets
Of festive freedom, and domestic ease,
With throbbing heart, to the stern discipline
Of pedagogue morose I sad return'd.

At school, he formed a friendship with the poet William Shenstone, and they exchanged letters and forthright criticisms of one another's poems throughout their lives (so forthright, in fact, that Shenstone once wrote to assure Jago that the poem *Edge-Hill* was worth finishing despite Shenstone's critical remarks about it). Jago went from school to University College Oxford, where he was a 'servitor': a student who received free accommodation (and some free meals), and was exempted from paying fees for lectures. At Oxford, servitors were also expected to act as servants to the fellows of their college. Jago followed his father into the church in 1737, and received his master's degree on July 9th, 1738. He served his curacy at Snitterfield, and must have made a good impression, as they later welcomed him back.

MARRIAGE AND A PERPETUAL CURACY

In 1740, his father died. Three or four years later, at the age of 29, he married Dorothea Susanna Fancourt, a vicar's daughter from Kilmcote in Leicestershire. He had known her since childhood, and Chalmers describes her as 'amiable and accomplished'.

They made their first home together in Harbury after he was presented with the living in 1746. Perhaps his poem *Delia* is a record of his love for her:

> *With leaden foot Time creeps along*
> *While Delia is away:*
> *With her, not plaintive was the song,*
> *Nor tedious was the day.*
> *Ah, envious Pow'r! Reverse my doom;*
> *Now double thy career,*
> *Strain ev'ry nerve, stretch ev'ry plume,*
> *And rest them when she's here!*

Shortly after, in 1749, Lord Willoughby de Broke added the 'perpetual curacy' of Chesterton to Harbury. The couple must have been grateful for the additional parish; the two benefices together did not produce more than a hundred pounds a year, and by 1751 he and Dorothea had seven

The village pump, just outside the church walls, would have been functional in Jago's day. Here Ted Crowley and Roland Hughes complete repairs.

children. So it was a great tragedy when Dorothea died in that year, and Richard was left to care for them all. 'From such a loss (he became) the most inconsolable widower'. His friends rallied round, and Lord Clare procured the vicarage of Snitterfield for him in 1754. He remained vicar of Harbury, and of Chesterton, too. He remarried four years later. His new wife, Margaret, the daughter of a Staffordshire gentleman, bore him no children, and in 1771, he followed his first father-in-law into the living of Kilmcote, where Dorothea grew up. This gave enough income, with Snitterfield, to maintain his family in 'ease and comfort'. So according to his biographer, he resigned the 'trifling' parish of Harbury. He might not have agreed with this dismissive description of his work in Harbury. The parish records show him baptising twenty to thirty babes a year, for example, and marrying local families whose names still resonate in the village – Biddle, Sabin, Sprawson. Many of them were sadly illiterate, signing the register with their mark. He lived out his life almost entirely at Snitterfield, amusing himself with improvements to the vicarage and garden. And of course, he wrote poetry.

EVERY COUNTRY SEAT – BUT HARBURY

'His rank as a poet cannot be thought very high' says Chalmers, quickly adding that 'we have few more beautiful specimens of tenderness and sensibility than in his *Elegies on the Blackbirds and Goldfinches*'. And his '*Blackbirds*' elegy was good enough for both another author, and the manager of the Bath Theatre separately, to claim it as their own. The theatre manager even claimed that Jago did not exist, and was a fictitious name he had taken from *Othello*.

But Jago had the confidence to write a parody of Hamlet's *Soliloquy*:

To print or not to print – that is the question.
Whether 'tis better in a trunk to bury
The quirks and crotchets of outrageous fancy,
Or send a well-wrote copy to the press,
And by disclosing, end them?

His interests were broad. Among other humorous pieces is an *Essay on Electricity* from 1759, now sadly lost. And the third book of *Edge-Hill* is a lengthy scientific discourse, too: on the theory of sight. *Edge-Hill* is

Jago's longest poem; he mentions 'every country seat of any importance in the county'. It was criticised as being geographically inaccurate: 'To enjoy it, the reader must have a map constantly before him'. Despite its considerable length, and inclusion of most of the towns and villages of South Warwickshire, it makes no mention of Harbury.

A CHURCHYARD GHOST AND A SERMON

According to the Warwick archives, this was the debatable event when a ghost was fired at, the bullet lodging itself in the door of the Wagstaffe School. Jago neither confirms nor questions the encounter, which has overtones of Scrooge and the ghost of Jacob Marley, but uses it as an opportunity to enforce the necessity of repentance.

The congregation was greatly exercised by the stories of this mysterious ghost. Tired of the rumours and gossip, Jago preached against dabbling in the supernatural. His sermon had the riveting subtitle: '*The Causes of Impenitence considered, As Well in the Case of Extraordinary Warnings as under the General Laws of Providential Grace*'. Jago took as his text 'For if ye hear not Moses and the prophets neither will ye be persuaded though one rise from the dead'. Believers in the supernatural were belaboured about 'chambering and wantonness' and called to seriousness and reformation - chambering being a more acceptable word for adultery.

Jago contrasted the fates of Dives – rich in this life, but in hell in the next – and Lazarus, a beggar on Earth, but 'in Abraham's bosom' after his death. One of the lessons of this parable is to accept the ordinary means of instruction or grace – and not to wait for, or expect 'extraordinary and supernatural providences'. After recalling the commandments, and warning of the results of neglecting them, he reminded his congregation, and later readers, that 'there remaineth a day in which the Heavens shall pass away with a great noise, and the elements shall melt with a great heat', when the 'perversely wicked will be for ever tormented'. 'Take warning in time. Wait for no other monitors' – no other guides to good behaviour. His threat must have worked. There is no record of a further mention of the ghost. Nor is there a record of continuing 'chambering and wantonness'. The sermon was published by George

Huddesford of Oxford on the 27th of May, 1755. The money from the sale of the sermon booklet was 'employed, along with other donations, for the Recovery of a Salary belonging to the Free-School in Harbury, which for some years past has been withheld from it'. Betty Smith, in her book *Ghosts of Warwickshire*, published in 1992, places the ghost very firmly in Chesterton, and indeed Jago wrote a fifteen-verse epic poem called *Peyto's Ghost* which she claims was inspired by the ghost in the neighbouring parish.

RICHARD JAGO, THE MAN

His biographer describes Jago as 'of middle stature; reserved among strangers, free and easy amongst his friends'. He records that 'by his doctrine and example, (he was) a faithful and worthy minister of the parish over which he presided'. It is not clear which of his parishes is referred to here; so let's be kind and assume that it was a general observation. It seems likely. In the preface to his poems, he shows great generosity of spirit, taking to task 'censorious Christians; whose disapproving practice is so injurious to their neighbours' repose', and 'so contrary to all the laws of civility and good manners'. With a sideswipe at the Inquisition, he champions freedom of thought and expression, and those 'whose minds are always open to the feelings of others'.

Richard Jago died after a short illness on May 8th, 1781, aged sixty-five, and was buried, as he had chosen, in a family vault in Snitterfield churchyard. Three of his daughters survived him. A tablet in St James the Great, Snitterfield, records a fiery preacher but a compassionate minister. Three silver birches were planted in the vicarage garden by his daughters.

∾ 1774 The clock ∾

THE FIRST TOWER CLOCKS had no faces. They told the time solely by striking; an invaluable aid for a population without clocks or watches. Clocks were common in churches, of course. In 1288, the precursor to Big Ben was hung in a clock tower in Westminster, and four years later, a clock was put in Canterbury cathedral. But it was some time before the advantages of a readable clock face, telling the time at a glance (if you were close enough), were generally realised. In 1744 a clock made by Charles Oldham was installed in All Saints. We know there was a previous clock since Oldham built and fitted his replacement for £18 – allowing £7 to retain the old clock against his total price of £25. There were two Charles Oldhams; one was apprenticed to William

Tom Hauley winds the clock in the 1970s

Wilks of Wolverton in 1763, and other Oldhams are recorded as War-wickshire clockmakers. (Interestingly, if you want historical details on clockmakers, the present web site is managed by an A Oldham). Charles worked in Southam and his craftsmanship is recorded by a bell sewn on the Southam Embroideries, displayed in the Grange Hall. He worked in the town from 1770 to 1830, and his beautiful long case clocks are still in demand. At the time of writing, one is for auction at Sothebys.

WINDING EVERY DAY

This original clock had to be hand wound every day, and for many years, church parishioners, including in recent years Tom Hauley, Peter Pryke and Harry Windsor, devotedly climbed the spiral stairs to draw the weights up the tower - Tom always accompanied by his faithful dog.

Then in 1994, money was raised by the ROC fund in the village to overhaul the clock and fit an electric drive to the winder. The overhaul cost twelve hundred pounds, with restoration of the face at a further nine hundred, but it was the conversion to mechanical winding – at nearly three thousand pounds – that released the winders from their daily task.

The gearing was reduced using Sturmey Archer bicycle gears. Neville Ellis made a case for the clock and panelling round the ringing chamber. He had previously whitewashed the inside of the ringing chamber, and he now panelled it. The table on which the clock stands is believed to be the same age as the clock. It tips a little, but still does the job.

∼ 1819 The Select Vestry ∼

A SELECT VESTRY is defined as 'a select number of persons cho-sen in large and populous English parishes to represent and manage the concerns of the parish for one year'. They managed local affairs including, crucially, the Poor Law. The chief source of local authority was the Justice of the Peace, and many clergymen became JPs. We don't know if any of our ministers had this dual role, which could be controversial.

The church around 1817 with a low pyramid-shaped roof, not a spire. The top part of the tower had been removed down to the ridge of the old nave. No door is shown on this, the south side. Possibly, like many churches and cathedrals, the original entrance was on the west side – the 'back' of the church

Harbury had a select vestry – all men, unsurprisingly – that met 'at the sign of the Dog' or sometimes at the New Inn, to distribute charity to the poor. In June, 1819, for example, the select vestry agreed to give shoes to 'Tom Lines's boy' (the shoes to be returned if he lost his job); in January 1820, a bedsheet to John Hixon, and five shillings to Elizabeth Shepherd 'to pay a midwife'. In May, 1820, the vestry appointed Mr Wright Loxton from Southam to give medical care to the poor of Harbury – and two families from neighbouring Bishop's Itchington. His fee was twenty-four pounds for the year; smallpox, cowpox, prescriptions and compound fractures extra. In 1826, it appointed Thomas Sprawson as village constable. The Victorian equivalent of the never-ending complaints about dogs fouling Harbury's pavements was the thistle problem. Thistles blocked the footpaths, making journeys on foot impossible. They are frequently discussed, and labourers dispatched to cut them down. Moles, however, were the responsibility of the churchwardens, to be caught at their expense.

In the 1851 census the vicar, the Reverend Clement Newsam, was living in Church Street. A widower aged 74 with 288 acres, he employed six labourers and two boys. Living next door was a farm bailiff, his wife and their three servants. There were two other dwellings in Church Street, one occupied by a doctor and family and the fourth being a grocers and drapers. Newsam is buried in the church, and his memorial, and a very moving one to Abraham Classon, were recently rehung in the choir vestry at the base of the tower.

On Easter Monday, 1852, without recorded explanation or ceremony, William Wight, Vicar, took the place of Parson Clement Newsam.

THE CHAPELS

The two non-comformist chapels were part of Harbury's worshipping community. The Wesleyan Chapel, now a private house in Chapel Street, opened in 1800, a year before the Methodist chapel in Warwick. In 1837, it was part of the Banbury circuit, with thirty members and its own burial ground. It had a significant preaching family. John Bustin and his son William giving up their Sundays to travel and preach.

The Primitive Methodist Chapel was in Mill Street, in the present Chapel House, just four houses up from the present medical centre. Miss Bird, who lived in Bird's Cottage in Mill Street – the house where she was born – recalled, in the *Harbury and Ladbroke News* of March, 1975, when both chapels, and the parish church, were well attended on a Sunday.

The accounts note that the chapel acquired a harmonium in 1877 at sixteen guineas, and had it repaired, ten years later, for five shillings. Sadly, the accounts end in 1904, when the chapel had a balance in hand of four shillings and one penny.

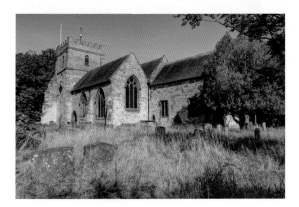

Harbury House and the bury from the bell tower.

Neville Ellis and Ralph Swadling with the new bell tower louvres they made in 2002 to the original design.
Jeff Bedford, project manager, looks on.

All Saints' Church 2012.

Peter Clarke with a bell from Winderton, 1981.

To the Glory of God
and in memory of
MATTHEW HARVEY HOLE;
BORN 22ND NOVEMBER 1824, DIED 9TH JUNE 1887,
FOR TWENTY TWO YEARS VICAR OF THIS PARISH,
DURING WHOSE MINISTRY
THE CHURCH WAS RESTORED AND GREATLY BEAUTIFIED;
THE ABOVE WINDOW HAS BEEN PLACED HERE
BY HIS PARISHIONERS AND NUMEROUS FRIENDS
ALL SAINTS DAY, 1ST NOVEMBER, 1890.

The window in the west wall depicting Christ the Shepherd is in memory of three children of Matthew Hole; Georgina, Arthur and John.

A memorial in the tower vestry to Abraham Classon, a 'constant attendant upon the service of the church'.

Memorial to Anne Wagstaffe.

ANNE WAGSTAF DAVGHT: TO IO: ...
OF STONITHORPE, HEARE DOTH LYE:
WHOSE VERTVOVS LIFE DID WELL DESERV
ETERNALL MEMORYE QVE OBBIIT
ANO DOMINI 1634

Richard Jago

Charles Oldham's clock, 1744.

The entrance to the church before the installation of the lych gate in 1910.

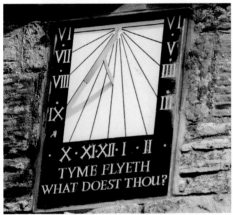

The new sundial in its place on the south tower buttress.

Memorial to Jacob Wright, 1685, set in the floor near the west wall.

The East Window is Victorian stained glass. The pictures show Jairus's daughter; Lazarus; the widow of Nain; and the entombment, Resurrection and Ascension of Jesus, with Christ in glory above. The Greek letters are IHC (IHCOYC – Jesus) and XPICTOC – Christ. The window is in memory of the Sabin and Heath families. (Photograph by David Steele)

～ 1852-1865 ～
William Wight
the 'model' minister

'Harbury is situated on a rising ground about 400 feet above the level of the sea and its salubrity is attested by the longevity of its inhabitants'.

From the Rules of the Harbury Schools, 1852

ABOVE THE DOOR of the Wight School is the inscription: 'Erected AD 1856; Rev. William Wight M.A. Vicar.' The Reverend William Wight, practical Christian, temperance advocate and humanitarian, left more than this mark on the village between 1852 and 1865. There

"Harbury church, Vicarage, &c." From a publication by William Wight.

53

Rev. William Wight M.A.

54

is no record of any marriage (although interestingly, he is described as a widower in records of his later life). In any event this dynamic man would appear to have had little time for a wife and family.

William Wight had been born in London, and according to an article written by local historian Celia Barrett, his pamphlet on poverty stated that 'one hundred thousand, on rising in the morning, did not know where they were going to sleep at night'. He was concerned that a hundred thousand young Londoners had no education, and a million and a half had never been to church.

Wight wanted to found an ideal society. He made up his mind to find a village in the centre of the country where he planned a social experiment: the making of a 'model parish'. But first, he had some wide-ranging experiences.

THE TEMPERANCE MOVEMENT AND IRELAND

Wight had a lifelong enthusiasm for temperance and the positive social effects of abstinence, and wrote commenting on the records of Father Mathew, who traveled through Great Britain, preaching against the demon drink. In *Temperance progress of the century*, William Wight confirms, after his own travels in Ireland, the positive effects of a sermon from Father Mathew from personal experience. A contemporary report reads:

The effects of (Father Mathew's) wonderful crusade were described as follows, in 1843, by the Rev. William Wight, M.A.:

'His ministry in Ireland alone, not counting (Father Mathew's) short trips to England and Scotland and his journey through America in 1849-1850, resulted in the pledging of three million people to total abstinence.

On inspecting prisons in Dublin, I was informed one was closed and for sale; in another I saw upwards of one hundred cells vacant; and in other jails, a similar state of things.

A friend who had visited Dublin prior to this movement, had led me to expect swarms of paupers would be besetting the steps of every respectable person's house; but on going over this fine city, little or nothing of the kind was visible.

THE MODEL BAZAAR.

To celebrate the opening of England's MODEL PARISH, it is intended, at the suggestion of some Christian friends, to have a BAZAAR,

ON THE VICARAGE GROUNDS,

IN AID OF THE FUND FOR ERECTING MODEL SCHOOLS.

Two children of the Parish, a boy and a girl, will be appointed to each stall, with ladies to superintend. Every article will have its price affixed to it, and no raffling will be allowed.

PATRONESSES:

HER GRACE THE DOWAGER DUCHESS OF NORTHUMBERLAND.
THE RIGHT HONOURABLE LADY WILLOUGHBY DE BROKE.
THE RIGHT HONOURABLE LADY LIFFORD.
THE RIGHT HONOURABLE LADY GUERNSEY.
LADY CHARLOTTE PALMER.   LADY CARNEGIE.
THE HONOURABLE MRS. CHARLES MOREWOOD.
MRS. BARNARD.   MRS. CHAMBERLAYNE.
ETC., ETC.

As the Oxford and Birmingham Railway, passes through the Parish, the place is of easy access from every part of the country.

☞ Friends visiting the BAZAAR will have an opportunity of seeing the great Railway Cutting in the Parish, supposed to be the *largest in the world!*

Contributions of Work, &c., may be sent per Rail to Harbury Vicarage, near Leamington.

Rev. Wight's Model Bazaar

At the great national banquet which took place in Dublin, Lord Morpeth, after giving the particulars of the returns of outrages in the constabulary office, by which it appeared that since 1836 they had diminished one-third, proceeded to remark that the heaviest offences, such us homicides, outrages upon the person, assaults with attempts to murder, aggravated assaults, cutting and maiming, were... most materially diminished.'

Clearly, temperance was the future, so for three years Wight travelled the country raising interest and looking for the perfect village to make teetotal; and in 1852 he accepted the living of Harbury.

Wight's aim was to improve the physical conditions in which Harbury people lived; to ensure that they had a sound moral character; and that they did not drink or smoke.

Social improvements

Perhaps as part of his introduction to the village, William Wight held a tea party in the vicarage grounds in July 1852.

It is claimed that over seven hundred attended the party, which, given the size of the village at that time, suggests a great hunger for a glimpse of the new Vicar, or perhaps for sandwiches and cake.

Later, at a Model Bazaar, 'two children of the parish, a boy and a girl, will be appointed to each stall, with ladies to superintend. Every article will have its price affixed to it, and no raffling will be allowed'. In a general advertisement for the event, Wight pointed out that the Oxford and Birmingham Railway passes through the parish, offering 'easy access from every part of the country'. Patronesses of the scheme included The Right Honourable Lady Willoughby de Broke and the Right Honourable Lady Guernsey'. The bazaar celebrated 'the opening of England's MODEL PARISH' and was 'IN AID OF THE FUND FOR ERECTING MODEL SCHOOLS'.

Afterwards, Wight wrote: 'The children, after an abundant supply of tea and cake, adjourned to the contiguous meadow, provided with traps (used for catching games), bats, balls, skipping ropes and other sources of healthy recreation, while the parents and friends sat down to their tea, after which they dispersed for games of cricket, archery and other active exercises, until distant peals of thunder and heavy masses of clouds gave an intimation of a coming storm which shortened the time allotted for the games'.

In true Wight style, a sign on the gate advised of 'No intoxicating liquors or smoking allowed in the grounds'.

Undeterred by the unreliable weather, Wight entertained a hundred navvies from the Railway Works later the same month. (You wonder how his housekeeper coped with all this hospitality.) He was struck by their surprisingly good behaviour, although he commented that 'It may not be unimportant to notice in all probability would the result of this evening have been, had beer or other intoxicating drinks been allowed'.

As it was, 'it was impossible to resist that, were means taken towards humanizing and improving their social position, an ample return would be the result' – presumably in the absence of drink.

A record of Vestry Meetings during Wight's incumbency was singularly dull and repetitive. He and other respectable householders met to select constables and 'Overseers of the poor'. It must have made a break to elect, in 1866, a Superintendent of highways. This worthy had his work cut out (at fifteen shillings a year) as he dealt with heavy use of the Southam and Kineton turnpike road, and demands from Elizabeth Sabin to 'stop up' a right of way passing near her house. The churchwardens were charged, annually, with 'mowing the thistles within the first fourteen days of July'. It made a break from the routine when, in 1871, the village constable (whose authority is unknown; he might have been a parish official) requested that a pair of handcuffs be provided. (Not that it made any difference; in a reflection of today, the committee complained in 1878 that there were 'disorders' on Sunday evenings since the village had no resident policeman.)

COTTAGES, ALLOTMENTS AND PRIZES

In 1853, Wight helped establish the 'Harbury Cottage Improvement Garden and Floricultural Association'. This was aimed at 'improved dwellings among the working classes, to secure greater attendance to cleanliness and to sanitary principles'. The new vicar offered prizes to 'respectable characters who attend a place of worship (interestingly, not just the parish church), who frequent no public house (of course not) and are guilty of no other degrading habits'. Further conditions of entry included freedom from debt or acceptance of parish relief, a healthy balance in a bank or building society and the ability to read and write. Clean-living villagers were given allotments, with the reward of an annual supper at which prizes were presented for gardening success. The Reverend Wight's five guineas were probably safe, since there would be no prizes for those who embrace the 'wasteful and dirty habit of smoking'.

Model cottages were rented out to those accepting no lodgers and with no plans to turn them into beer or tobacco shops. A Moral Police patrolled the village between nine and twelve at night to 'visit places of

The archway of the Wight School

resort and observe the state of the parish'.

Wight was still a great party-giver. In 1853, an 'Annual Dinner of the Harbury Octogenarians' took place in the vicarage grounds. The older schoolgirls, in pretty dresses, waited on the elderly villagers, serving them roast beef and plum pudding, and 'the cup that cheers but does not inebriate'. The weather was fine, and, after a hymn and Bible reading, the octogenarians made their sober way home.

WIGHT AND THE NATIONAL SCHOOL

> *The Rev William Wight, vicar of the parish of Harbury… on part of the Glebe land… to permit the said premises to be used as a school for the education of children and adults, or children only of the labouring, manufacturing and other poorer classes in the Parish of Harbury and for no other purpose.*

Conveyance of land for a school.

William Wight was enthusiastic about education, organizing evening classes on three nights a week, and a Model Library of three hundred volumes, but with 'no works of fiction or of a questionable character'.

But it is the school building – now a community library and coffee shop – that is his lasting monument.

By the middle of the nineteenth century, the average attendance at the old Wagstaffe School was fifty; Joseph West was schoolmaster. With the arrival of William Wight, the school changed its character, becoming the village infant school. In 1971, its school service over, the building was sold as a private house.

The National Society was the driving force for new schools across the country. It had been founded on October 16th 1811 as the 'National Society for Promoting the Education of the Poor in the Principles of the Established Church in England and Wales'. Its aim was that 'the National Religion should be made the foundation of National Education, and should be the first and chief thing taught to the poor, according to the excellent Liturgy and Catechism provided by our Church.' At the local level, National Schools were founded by the local vicar and members of the Church of England. William Wight applied to the Bishop of Worcester for support and in 1856, opened Harbury's own National School. Infants were still educated in the Wagstaffe school, which was eventually restored in 1866. But older children attended the 'Wight School'.

BOOKS, SLATES, MAPS, &C
WILL BE PROVIDED FREE OF ANY CHARGE

Wight's intentions went beyond those of the National Society. The Harbury school was to educate village children and 'bring them up in the Christian Spirit'. But the curriculum was driven by employment needs, and some of the education was vocational. The school attempted to 'combine industrial training with the intellectual courses of instruction (sic) to prepare the children for the duties of public and private life and to qualify some for the office of teachers and other employment and some for domestic service'. To this end, 'the first class girls will, three days in the week, be instructed at the Vicarage, by efficient servants, in household duties'. Wight may have been a philanthropist, but he kept a clean house. The school was clean, too: 'two of the labourers' children will, in rotation, have each evening to clean the schools, and to leave them prepared for the next day's duties'.

The rules of The Harbury School. recorded in 1852, assured parents that 'Books, Slates, Maps, &c will be provided free of any charge'. However, 'any child coming to school dirty or with uncombed hair will be sent back. Any child found guilty of dirty habits – bad language or any improper conduct, and persisting in such conduct after having been duly admonished, will be expelled the schools'. To 'secure the school from interruption, no person will be allowed to visit it without an order from the Vicar, who daily inspects the schools himself'. Wight also had plans for boarders who would be 'carefully kept from all evil companionship – from all contact with any drinking or smoking practices'.

School fees were set on a sliding scale, depending on the financial circumstances of the family. The first child of farm labourers was educated for the sum of two pence; succeeding children for one penny. The scale for 'mechanics' started at three pence, and for tradesmen at four. The children of 'Professional Men', and 'those in affluent circumstances' rose to ten shillings a quarter. The lancet windows of the Wight School are in typical Victorian schoolroom style, high enough to let in the light but not let the children see out and be distracted from their lessons. Even today, although the building has been sensitively updated, it is possible to stand in the 'Wight School' and imagine the children arriving with their school fees and a lump of coal for the stove.

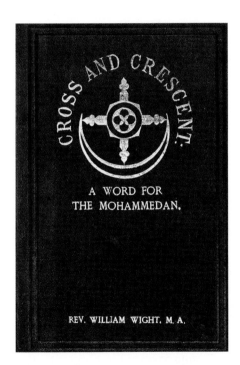

Cross and Crescent. A Word for the Mohammedan in the Present War, by William Wight. Published in 1877

A NOVEL ENTERTAINMENT

Wight's passionate belief in social justice and self-advancement is reflected in his comment on the School Treat of 1853, when the children were presumably still being educated in the Wagstaffe School. 'It should be stated that everyone contributed something towards the expenses of the trip, and thus they were agents in forwarding their own improvement and enjoyment'.

The children went to Kenilworth by train, to eat and play games. 'The day was most propitious and few excursions perhaps were ever more thoroughly enjoyed by all parties. To the children it was a novel entertainment, most of them never having been before in a railway carriage in their lives.' (An observation that Wight might make about many children today.)

William Wight left the living in 1865, and from 1878 to 1884 he lived, presumably in retirement, at a house called 'The Arab's Tent' in Chislehurst, where he died.

As it turned out, his building of the Wight School was propitious in more ways than one. Twenty years later, it was called into service as a temporary place of worship.

WRITER AND PUBLISHER

William Wight was an energetic writer on many subjects, and set up a printing press in Harbury – The Model (of course!) Printing and Binding Factory – to publish his works. In 1852, for example, he produced three books. *England's homes or, the dwellings of Englishmen*; *England's gin palaces, public houses and beer shops*, and *England's magistracy and clergy* (reflecting his continuing interest in temperance); and *A voice to the working classes; or, Who are their oppressors?* - all printed in Harbury.

Is the gospel a failure for England's people? or, Human exertion essential to human redemption: a sermon preached at the visitation of the Archdeacon of Coventry, at Southam, July 25th 1861, was published by Wertheim, Macintosh and Hunt in the same year.

Never one to be without an opinion, Wight travelled in what we now call the Middle East, and later expressed his views on the Russo-Turkish

War of 1877-1878. *Cross and Crescent. A Word for the Mohammedan in the Present War*, was published in 1877. It was subtitled *With reminiscences of travel in Mohammedan countries*.

Last Will and Testament

Appropriately for such a fighter, the last record of Wight's life is the contesting of his generous but eccentric will, reported in New Zealand's *Timaru Herald*, of the 17th Kohitatea (January) 1889 – a will that was contested by his heir on the grounds of Wight's insanity. His testament neatly sums up his benevolence, practically and response to the needs of others. The newspaper article reads:

'Mr Justice Chitty had before him recently on further consideration the will of the late Rev. William Wight, of the Arab's Tent, Chislehurst, formerly vicar of Harbury. By his will, he desired to found a

college for ladies – to train ladies for the important duties of wives, mistresses, and mothers. Women, he asserted in his will, should be something more useful and more noble than a pretty doll, a butterfly, or a plaything for their husband. To this end he provided for early rising of the ladies of the college, and for cold baths in the morning. He also provided for quarterly conversaziones, and directed that two thirds of the invitations should be sent to single gentlemen. He directed that he himself should be buried in his garden, near the grave of his noble Labrador dog 'Friend'.'

Wight had instructed that the surplus rents of houses he owned in Chiselhurst and Cheltenham should be accumulated until a sum of £10,000 was reached, then invested in Government securities to build this institution for young women. But the law must have its way, and the will probably fell foul of the perpetuity rules. Although Wight was not proved insane, the will was declared void, possibly under the so-called beneficiary principle. No 'Wight's Social and Domestic College for Young Ladies' was established, so ladies were denied their cold baths and male company:

> 'These bequests turned out to be illegal, and Mr Justice Chitty made an order giving specific directions as to the distribution of the property among the next of kin.'

He was recalled by the Reverend J R Macduff, his neighbour in Chislehurst and best selling author on the Victorian virtue of death and sorrow. A Kent amateur historian who lives in the same road as the Arab's Tent, Joanna Friel, reports that Macduff said of his neighbour:

> 'Among many kind friends at Chislehurst, it would be invidious to select. Not a few have already passed to the silent land. Among the latter I recall one of my nearest neighbours, a retired clergyman of the Church of England – Rev. Wm Wight: kind, sympathetic, hospitable, despite very pronounced eccentricities, which all his acquaintances understood, excused, and condoned. He had been during his life, and, indeed, to the last, a great traveller, specially in Egypt, Arabia, and Syria, which impelled him, by the force of these same eccentricities, to give his spacious house the name 'The Arab's Tent' - the penalty for which indiscretion he had, of course, himself to pay, by being called 'The Arab'. He had the singular and fortunate aptitude for gathering many nice, and some distinguished, people around him, literary, artistic, secular, sacred. He could even bag an Eastern Patriarch or a Bishop of Jerusalem, or a home church dignitary, or a Times correspondent, or such a celebrity as Mr Rassam of Nineveh and Babylonish fame, whom he brought to spend a pleasant evening here. Alas! The old Oriental phrase, 'O King, live for ever', could secure no exception in the case of my genial friend. I wrote the inscription for his tomb, now in Chislehurst churchyard.'

Despite his request, Wight was finally buried in St Nicholas Church graveyard in Chislehurst, Kent. There is some comfort here, since although Wight was not buried alongside his dog, an epitaph to 'Friend' was carved on its entrance. The grave reads: 'Rev. William WIGHT formerly vicar of Harbury, Warwickshire lately resident in Lower Camden, Chislehurst. Obiit 16 Oct 1884 obdormivit in Christo. Aged 74 years.'

∿ 1865-1887 Matthew Hole ∿ and church restoration

MATTHEW (sometimes 'Mathew') Hole was born, the son of a farmer, in Caunton, Nottinghamshire on November 22nd, 1824. He attended Grantham and Newark Grammar Schools before entering St John's College, Cambridge and taking a First Class degree in the Cambridge Classical Tripos. Emerging with his MA, he became a deacon and later a priest, was later curate of St John's Notting Hill, and lived in Kensington. Perhaps it was there that he met Caroline Hudson, who had been born the year after him, in Calcutta. They married at St John's on 29th June, 1854.

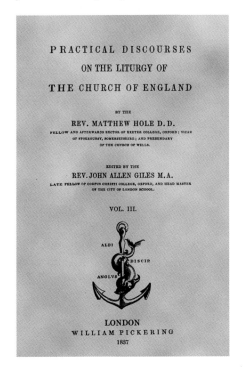

PRACTICAL DISCOURSES

ON THE LITURGY OF

THE CHURCH OF ENGLAND

BY THE

REV. MATTHEW HOLE D. D.

FELLOW AND AFTERWARDS RECTOR OF EXETER COLLEGE, OXFORD ; VICAR
OF STOKEGURSY, SOMERSETSHIRE ; AND PREBENDARY
OF THE CHURCH OF WELLS.

EDITED BY THE

REV. JOHN ALLEN GILES M.A.

LATE FELLOW OF CORPUS CHRISTI COLLEGE, OXFORD, AND HEAD MASTER
OF THE CITY OF LONDON SCHOOL.

VOL. III.

ALDI

DISCIP

ANGLVS

LONDON

WILLIAM PICKERING

1837

A Matthew Hole publication

Hole combined the priesthood with a teaching career, and in 1854/55, the 'Rev M H Hole' applied, unsuccessfully, for the Headmastership of Tewkesbury Grammar School. He had better luck at Alford in Lincolnshire where he became headmaster, and later he was Curate of Willoughby near Rugby for nine years. In 1865, he and Caroline and their growing family moved to Harbury despite (or possibly because of) its dilapidated church and poor parish. At that time, the gross income of the church was estimated at £380 per annum, but had 'greatly fallen off in consequence of the depreciation of the glebe' – the land belonging to, and part funding, the church. It was during his time in Harbury that the major rebuild of the church took place that leaves it as we see it today. It may be that he had significant income of his own that he ploughed into the project, possibly from his father's will.

The 1871 census records the family living in Church Street, and while two of their children appear to be living away, Catherine (15), the splendidly named Herbert Augustus (11), Henry (6) and Douglas (4) were at home. Another Catherine, Caroline's Aunt and an officer's widow, also from Calcutta and aged 72, lived with them. So did Anne Lockwood (aged 26) the children's governess, and four servants, including one from Ufton and another from Long Compton. The census records the parish as having 1,121 inhabitants at the time. By 1881, the family was still living in Church Street. Aunt Catherine was no longer with them, or possibly even with us.

Matthew Hole was minister at All Saints for twenty-one years in total, though the *Leamington Spa Courier* records that for the last two years of his life, he had never been 'strong and well, but has managed to perform the duties which devolved upon him'. Indeed, the *Courier* records that the Sunday before his death he had 'preached with much earnestness, and in his usual eloquent manner'. He died about 11 o'clock the following Thursday morning, an event 'not altogether unexpected, but somewhat sudden at the last. The greatest sympathy is manifested in the village for Mrs Hole and the family in their bereavement'. He died on June 9th, 1887.

His death left a gap that was filled by a number of other ministers before the appointment of Michail Kearney. Matthew Hole wrote widely on the liturgy and catechism, and some of his books are still in print. Matthew Hole was remembered in the *Courier* for his kindness, his courtesy and his numerous friends. 'He was a consistent Conservative in politics, but never allowed his political views to offend his parishioners'

1865 Letter from Matthew Hole

On Christmas Day, 1865, the Reverend Matthew Hole, Vicar of Harbury, wrote to his parishioners. A copy of this printed letter, neatly folded into a bond envelope and addressed in a sloping hand to Miss or Mrs

Spraggett, is in the County Records Office. It concerns 'matters relating to the welfare of the parish on which I cannot conveniently address you (the parishioners) from the pulpit'.

The letter concerned the church accommodation, a problem that would eventually lead to major rebuilding work. While the church was

The architect's plan of 1871 included a spire

well-attended, accommodation in the church was 'not sufficient', and parishioners were asked to do what they could to let others share the available space. The Reverend Hole appealed for devout and reverent behaviour in the House of God – and asked parishioners never to be late, a practice which 'unfits your mind for devotion, and disturbs the prayers of others'.

The collection made every month for the poor amounted to £7 4s. 10d. The Reverend Hole 'expended it to the relief of the poor and necessitous' to the best of his ability. A Coal Club was to be added to the Clothing

Club, which received the savings of 140 families of the 'industrious poor'.

The Reverend Hole agreed that the Wagstaffe School should remain an infant school, with a trained schoolmistress, to prepare poor children for the National School and 'the diligent superintendence of its present excellent master'. He asked that children were sent neat and clean. Grubby children were likely to get short shrift. 'Help, let me say in passing, is unwillingly given where dirt prevails, for it is too sure a proof of idleness and mismanagement'. He assured parishioners that his door was 'always open to speak on any matter that concerns your interests, and I am generally at home from 10 to 11'.

Finally, he turned to those 'who neglect religion altogether'. He pointed out that 'who may be taken from the midst of us before the year is finished, none can tell; when it has passed, familiar faces will be missed from our parish, some of whom will be little expecting the summons. It may be *you.*' (The Reverend Hole's italics). He went on to 'press upon you that you seek the Saviour; each year carries with it the record of how we have spent it, *and that record is kept.*'

No wonder the church was well attended.

∾ 1872 The church rebuilt ∾

'The present Church is dark and incommodious ....Vexatious disputes have from time to time arisen.'

THE VICTORIAN RESTORATION

On the 11th of April, 1871, the *Minute Book of the Vestry Meetings of All Saints* records that 'The proposed restoration of the Parish Church and the plans of Mr Buckeridge the architect were laid before the meeting by the Vicar and Churchwardens'. As a result, the Vicar and Churchwardens were 'empowered to apply for a Faculty (Diocesan permission) for the rebuilding of the church whenever in their opinion the required funds are raised'. In fact, fund-raising moved apace. Six months later, on the 5th of October, the Vestry Meeting in the Wagstaffe School Room was advised that 'the sum of Three thousand three hundred pounds has been promised by the landowners and parishioners and other promoters of the work'. Among these 'promoters' may have been the Reverend Matthew Hole himself. A schedule of the monuments and gravestones had been prepared, ready for their removal. Permission was needed to open graves and disinter bodies. 'As far as the representatives of the deceased could be ascertained, (their) consent had been obtained'. The monuments and gravestones would be placed either on the walls of the church or along the north walls of the churchyard 'with the full approval of the representatives aforesaid'. All was ready for the great restoration job, the estimated expense of which was 'Three thousand four hundred pounds or thereabouts'. The collection was only a hundred pounds short of its target – always allowing that the job was brought in on budget.

A REQUEST TO THE DIOCESE

At the time, Harbury was in the Diocese of Worcester. So a copy of the April minutes were presented to the Lord Bishop of Worcester on the 20th of January, 1872, accompanied by 'Ground plans of the present Seats in the Church and the proposed new Seats'.

The request was formal and courteous, following a standard form. This was a period of furious controversy on the layout of churches. There were several great Privy Council cases. This plan apparently didn't upset anyone. It read: 'Your Petitioners humbly pray that you will be pleased to decree a licence or Faculty for

The present octagonal pulpit, installed during the 1872 rebuild

the purposes aforesaid provided no sufficient cause be shown to the contrary'. The petition was signed by the churchwardens, William Walls and William Seymour King, and by the Vicar, Matthew Harvey Hole, MA. The petition explained that 'the Inhabitants of Harbury wish to restore and enlarge the Parish Church and to increase the accommodation by renewing the Galleries and all existing Seats, reseating and reflooring the Church, new roofing, adding a New Aisle and Vestry Chamber on the North side of the same'.

This view of the Victorian church shows a door in the tower, and a canopy over the south door

There was no doubt in their minds that the church building was in poor shape. 'The present Church is dark and incommodious and does not provide adequate accommodation for the Parishioners, and that for want of such accommodation many do not attend the Services of the Church and that vexatious disputes (presumably rows over the few decent seats) have from time to time arisen'.

The tower was still giving trouble. Earlier in the century, it had been topped with brick, giving the impression of castle battlements. But it had finally settled, and was now supporting its buttresses, rather than the other way around.

By the 5th of March, 1872, it was agreed that the 'said chancel of the Parish Church of Harbury... may be restored, reseated and refitted and that such portion of the North Wall of the said Chancel as may be sufficient for the insertion of an arch connecting the said Chancel with the said New Vestry and Organ Chamber may be taken down'. The faculty was signed by Louise Ryland, John Seaman, Elizabeth Sabin and Edward

Mann. Among the witnesses were Edwin Teaman, a Harbury farmer, John Sabin Smith, a Lieutenant in the 45th Regiment and a resident of 'Ladbrooke', and Caroline Margaret Hole, the vicar's wife.

The document was circulated, signed and witnessed within two days. The work was urgently needed.

In the meantime, where were church services to be held? On the 29th of June, 1872, 'Henry, by Divine Permission Bishop of Worcester' granted to 'Matthew Harvey Hole, Clerk (In Holy Orders) MA ... and to his 'Curate or Curates lawfully Nominated and Licenced, Our Licence and authority to Officiate in the National School Room'. Services would take place in the 'Wight School' throughout the building as long as 'every Baptism shall at the time of its celebration be registered in the Registry of Baptisms'. The document, is signed 'H Worcester' in its margin, and sealed with the bishop's seal.

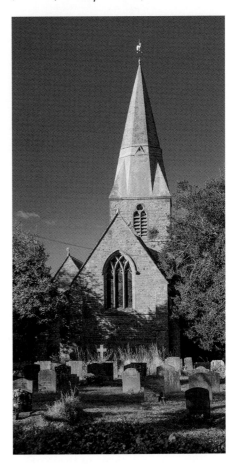

RESTORING THE CHURCH

The architect for the restoration, Charles Buckeridge, had offices in both Cavendish Square in London and more locally at St Aldate's in Oxford. He died before the building was completed. His specification for the work, addressed to Matthew Hole, was detailed and thoughtful.

Mr Buckeridge had built a similar spire in Radway

The church interior, pre 1875, with box pews – one where the pulpit now stands – and a rood screen. The memorial at the front is to Abraham Classon – now in the bell tower vestry. A photographer is recorded as staying at the Crown Inn in the 1860s , photographing the railway cutting and the church. Possibly this is one of his.

Some old materials would be recycled. It was agreed that the contractor would take away the old materials that could not be used, allowing for them in his price. He apparently did not want one of the windows – or sold it on – as its rubble reputedly became a rockery at Wissett Lodge, opposite the church.

The attention to detail in the job specification is impressive. The church was approached with great care – the stonework to be 'thoroughly restored with stone of the same description as the old'. The mortar was to be of 'fresh burnt blue Lias lime and Hitchington sand of the best quality in proportions of three of sand to one of lime'. The windows, cappings and south doorway were all to be of Hornton stone; the north arcade and arches into the vestry to be of Warwick stone. A lot of the filling material for the stonework probably came from Harbury quarry. It would have been 'overburden' – the first few feet of rock before the rock or limestone.

Some of it came from the demolished manor house (one of four or five in the village) that stood where the Victorian, brick-built Chesterton House Farm is now in Mill Street. The builders were employed by Messrs. J and T Davis of Banbury. An interesting anomaly is the centre outside window frame on the north aisle, which is the only one made of sandstone. Possibly it is an earlier frame, recycled. The old roof timbers of the nave were cleaned, repaired and restored. The original hammer beams were retained. The chancel roof was untouched. The rafters were new, of 5" by 4" English oak, and oak was used for the porch. The doors were made of pitch pine, and the princely sum of fifteen pounds was put aside for latches, locks and hinges. Sixty pounds was allowed for the screens in 'best Riga wainscot oak'.

An archway was cut out to accommodate the organ. A door was cut into the tower. The south aisle window behind the altar was built up with stone. When the church's wood block floor was relaid in 2011, a stone paving was found 30cm – about a foot – below the present one. There is no evidence that this is the original floor of the medieval church or that the floor was raised by this amount. The tiles were 4.5 inches plain at six shilling a yard, and those in the chancel, 10 and 20 shillings a yard, the lily design being the most expensive. The glass in the windows was in

The Heath family are remembered by a window

21oz Bristol sanded sheet glass 'of approved tint'. All the ironwork in the church was given four coats of a good oil paint. The altar cost fifteen pounds; the pulpit, thirty-five. Ten pounds paid for the lectern, and thirty-five, the new font and cover. The old font had been condemned by the Archdeacon in 1828 as too shallow and 'quite improper'. 'Warming' – perhaps the pipes along the aisles, now sunk below floor level – cost sixty pounds.

Any human remains that were found were collected and reburied under the direction of the vicar. Tombs and gravestones were protected. The windows in the North wall were to be removed with great care, cleaned, stacked and refixed 'in a perfect state'. The church was restored to the written specification, with 450 seats 'all free and unappropriated'. The lower part of the tower was restored as a baptistry – a place where baptisms were held. The final cost was four thousand pounds: equivalent to about a quarter of a million pounds today. Faculties seldom move that quickly in the twenty-first century. While the cost of rebuilding was largely met by subscription, Miss Ryland of Barford generously gave a thousand pounds - over sixty thousand pounds at today's values. Not all the plans were followed. He devised a very large wooden gable cross for the chancel, never built. The architect's original design also shows a church with an ornate spire. In the event, there were not the funds to construct the spire, and it was completed as we see it now, still with its brick top. Inside, the plaster was stripped from the walls and the bare stone was exposed. The specification requires distemper – a water-based paint mixed with glue, egg yolk or white – to be scraped from the walls. Plain tiles from Coopers of Maidenhead (No 2 pattern) were used for the roof, serving the church well until 1979, when repairs were put in hand funded in part with a substantial donation from Ethel Sollis in memory of her builder husband, Tony, who had worked on the church himself. The church was rewired and a sound system fitted, as well as the roof repairs.

THE LYCHGATE

The main gate into the churchyard was once halfway along the front wall onto Church Street. It was replaced by the lychgate facing the south door. The original Lychgate in memory of Mary Pearman dated from 1910 (a Faculty or permission to build was granted on 6th April, 1910) and it was rebuilt in January and February 1992 using grants from both the Parish Council and Stratford District Council. Most of the

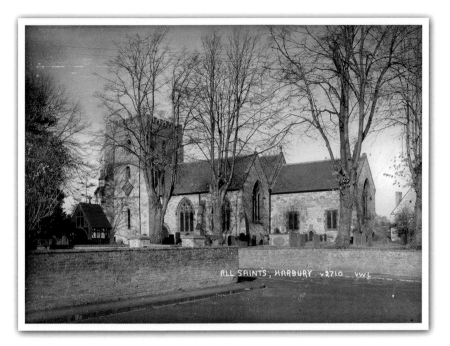

All Saints' Harbury and lych gate

wood was beyond repair, so Ashley and Sons of Bulkington copied the original structure in wood, incorporating the dedication. The gate was rededicated on March 1st, 1992.

Its small roof covers the entrance gate to the churchyard. Its name comes from *lic*, the Old English for corpse, because it was a shelter for the coffin and pallbearers before they entered the church for a funeral. The priest would come out and meet the coffin; originally, he needed the legal certificate for a burial from the relatives of the deceased. Nowadays, it is more of a courtesy to conduct the coffin into church.

Church Street adjoining the spinney is unusually wide. There are several possibilities. This may have been for carriages to turn after delivering worshippers to church. It may have allowed carriages to turn in for a driveway to the vicarage, though it faces Wissett Lodge rather than the site of the vicarage stables. It may have been intended to give access into what is now the spinney area. There were trees in that location at the end of the 19th century shown on a map from about 1905.

The lych gate was renovated in 1992

In 1873, the Misses Hill, owners of the land on the north and west sides of the churchyard, demanded, and got, a door in the wall of the church near the northwest corner; presumably the door that now opens into the Tom Hauley Room.

Six hundred bricks were ordered, for repairs to a house in the church-yard. Early maps show a building in the centre of the field next to the church. Whether this was a house – possibly an early vicarage – is speculative. There is evidence of a capped well in the spinney, which might have served this building. The house can be seen in some illustrations of the time, but it doesn't appear on OS maps, while the well does. No trace of the structure remains.

A NEW FLOOR

As part of the 1872 extensions to the church a pine wood block floor was laid. There was little wear on the floor over the next 120 years, but the floor was laid without a suitable damp proof membrane and by the end of the 20th century many areas were affected by wet rot from the concrete screed beneath, causing blocks to become loose and uneven.

In 2011 the new floor was laid using western red cedar blocks sourced from a cedar tree grown in the grounds of an earlier Coventry Hospital. The tree had been felled and stored and seasoned for approximately five years. The floor was laid with a liquid bituminous damp proof membrane on the original lime-concrete screed.

During these repairs to the original concrete subfloor, evidence was uncovered of the stone floor approximately 30cm below the existing floor, and in the north aisle builders found the stumps of wooden scaffold poles left in the ground after the 1872 extensions.

At the same time, the high pressure heating pipes laid around 1908 were replaced and lowered into ducts formed in the tiled areas of nave, aisles and transepts of the church.

The cost of the timber floor replacement was approximately £22,000 with a further £15,000 to replace the heating pipes. The project manager for the works was Jeff Bedford.

∼ 1873 The Cemetery ∼

I N 1873, the need for an additional burial ground became clear. A practically-titled Burial Board was appointed. An acre and a half of grounds would be needed; a chapel and gravel walks. A covered gateway was planned with 'a small room as a receptacle for a dead body'. This was a pragmatic response to the small size of houses at the time. A family might be living cheek by jowl with a corpse until the interment; and the body might be a source of infection. Better it was in the 'house of the dead'.

A plan was drawn up for the cemetery on the corner of South Parade. The area was bordered by the arable farm of Miss Russell and the market garden of Mr Startin.

The finances of the Vestry Committee were not in good shape. At one point they were seventeen pounds in debt. So it was agreed that

seven hundred pounds would be
needed. Estimates for the work
were land at three hundred pounds,
a chapel at four hundred pounds,
gravel paths at one hundred
pounds, and a hundred
pounds for conse-
cration and sun-
dries. It's not
surprising
that the
house
of the
dead was abandoned.

The cemetery planned in 1873

Harbury's was only one
of many cemeteries set up
around the country at this
time, separate from church-
yards. They served the in-
creasing population, and sadly, the growing number of deaths resulting
from poor public hygiene. The space in a church graveyard was at a
premium, and there was a general resistance in many churches to the
demand to bury any parishioner, especially those who had never dark-
ened the door of the church itself.

On the 12th of February, 1874, Mr R Lowe sanctioned the division
of Harbury Cemetery into 'three fourths to be consecrated, and one
fourth to be left unconsecrated'. Presumably this is Robert Lowe, Home
Secretary from 1873 to 1874.

Before 1880 nobody could be buried in consecrated ground except
following a Church service, which the minister of the parish or a person
authorized by him was bound to perform. So the division of the cemetery
probably reflected the substantial congregations at the non-conformist
chapels in Harbury. Every parishioner had the right of burial within his
parish, but while Anglican churchgoers were welcome in the consecrated
ground, non-conformists were buried in the non-consecrated area of
the cemetery – together with suicides of any denomination.

∿ Victorian times ∿
ministers and developments

Wight school pupils 1880

1806-1852 CLEMENT NEWSAM

The Reverend Clement Newsam, MA, his wife Hannah and two of their children, James and Laura, who died in infancy, are remembered by a wall tablet in the church, together with another Clement Newsam who died in Madras in 1842 and a daughter Frances Maria who died in 1844.

1887-1891 MICHAIL OR MICHAEL NEVILLE KEARNEY

Our Irish minister, born in County Tyrone about 1848, gained his MA degree at Trinity College, Dublin and married an Englishwoman, Edith Manby from Morecambe, on 6th February, 1878. He had already been a minister in Ireland. The Rev. Michael Neville Kearney, MA, was appointed to the incumbency of St. John's Cloverhill, diocese of Kilmore, by the patron of the living, S Sanderson, Esq. in 1871. It appears that his patron at All Saints was his wife, Edith Kearney, and he was minister from 1897-1922 under her patronage. They arrived with two children, Eardly (born in Roscommon, Ireland) and Hector, and added a Michail of their own while they were in Harbury. Penelope Major boarded with them. Penelope was born in Ireland too, older than both of them and apparently related – for Hector's full name was Hector Aemon Major Kearney. They lived at the Vicarage, which was still at 25 Church Street, and had two servants with local names: Fanny Overton, aged 18 and Gertrude Bird, aged 15, at the time of the 1891 census.

1891-1897 MORTIMER LINKLATER, THE ARCHITECT VICAR

The Reverend Mortimer Linklater, minister from 1891-1897

Mortimer Linklater was born in Blackrock, Dublin, probably in 1842. For the 1881 census, he was boarding with the Astill family in Leicester St Margaret, while he was curate at St Matthew's. But in 1891, he and his wife, Fanny, whom he had married in 1882, were recorded at the vicarage in Church Street, Olney, where his brother-in-law, John P Langley, was minister. Fanny was the daughter of Nathanial Stone, a Land Agent. They may have been visiting the Reverend Langley, as 1891 was the year Linklater became vicar of All Saints.

His career was varied. Linklater was educated at Portswood School in Southampton and at Great Malvern School, and then went to Chichester College in 1875. He qualified as an architect, becoming an Associate of the Royal Institute of British Architects, and was ordained in 1877. He was first curate of Croxton Kernel in Leicestershire, then of St Neot's, Cambridgeshire and of St Matthew's church, Leicester and finally of Horspath in South Oxfordshire.

In 1881, he became vicar of Rowley Regis in what is now Sandwell, and ten years later he moved to Harbury, where he stayed until 1897.

Mortimer was replaced in Harbury by John Beardsworth, and in 1901, at the age of 59, he and Fanny, then aged 51, were living or lodging in 16a Warrior Square, Hastings St Mary Magdalen. By 1911, they had moved to Church Road,

The Reverend John Beardsworth, minister from 1897-1922

St Leonards. Mortimer Linklater died in Hastings in 1923 at the age of 81, and Fanny died three years later.

BETWEEN EARTH AND HEAVEN: THE FONT

The medieval font was first replaced by the Georgian font, which was later moved from the church and stands outside between the west buttresses of the tower. It is described in Pevsner's *Buildings of England* as 'Georgian; a tapered pillar; the bowl is very small and just sunk into the top'. The present font was first at the traditional place at the back of the church, by the north door. Here, it represented the starting point on life's journey. You could imagine that journey, trekking up through the nave to the chancel.

This font is octagonal in shape. This is a compromise between two shapes: the perfect circle representing heaven, and the four-sided square, representing Earth. The octagon, then, is between the two shapes. When

The Georgian font and the new, octagonal, font

we are baptised, the font hold us between Earth and heaven.

The new font was later pressure-washed by Andrew Clarke, and moved from its original place by the north door to its present place at the front of the church on 10th November, 1990, when the Tom Hauley Room was built.

THE CRYPT

In the early 1950s, George Marshall, a local builder, was repairing the chancel floor when he broke though into a large underground room about the size of the chancel itself. This is the crypt of the church, defined as 'an underground vault or chamber, especially one beneath a church that is used as a burial place'. He discovered a lead coffin about seven feet long, surrounded by five other coffins, three of them clearly those of children. The coffins had family crests which had deteriorated so badly they could not be identified. It was suggested that they were from the Wagstaffe family, and had been moved there from a graveyard area below the north aisle when that was built in the 1800s. The floor was relaid, and the coffins left to rest in peace.

1883 THE NEW ORGAN

By 1848, the church's music was provided by a small organ. But in 1883, this was replaced by a splendid new church organ. The new organ was built by Thomas Atterton, part of an organ-building family established in 1857 and working until 1920 at 11 High Street, Leighton Buzzard. It was put in 'at the expense of the Reverend Clement Newsam, Vicar of Harbury, and Mr Sabin'.

At 3.30 pm on Queen Victoria's birthday, Thursday, May 24th, 1883, the new church organ was 'opened'. A sermon was preached by the vicar, the 'Reverend Canon Hole'. The collection was in aid of the Organ Fund, and a 'public tea' followed, with tickets at 9d. each, and 6d. for under tens – who possibly ate more! This was a popular event, and 'early application' was requested. Flowers in pots ('to be returned') were requested to decorate the church, these having 'proved very effective in the windows on previous occasions'.

The Victorian pews were guaranteed free of charge – by law

In 1884, the new organ was improved by 'the extension of the Cornopean stop', which gave a trumpet-like tone. But by 1921, the organ was badly in need of repair, and a garden social was arranged in aid of organ funds. It was the organist, Mr L Huggins, who donated the bulk of this money – a princely seventy-five pounds, which outweighed the twenty-eight pounds, three shillings and eleven pence ha'penny raised by collections. Fortuitously, the repaired organ narrowly escaped damage in the January gales the following year. Although the stone cross on the top of the church was blown down, damaging the tiles above the vestry, the organ was unharmed.

In September, 1993, the ROC fund was inaugurated, for work on the Roof, Organ and Clock. The overhaul of the organ was estimated at twenty thousand pounds. By the following January, it already stood at £2,800 when a gift day boosted it by a further £6,500.

∽ 1922-1930 ∽
Pierre Wolfe Daimpre

Pierre Wolfe Daimpre

DAIMPRE was vicar of Harbury from 1922 to 1930, and was 'Remembered by all his friends here with affection and gratefulness' (the then minister the Reverend A F Capps recording his death in the parish news of August, 1940). Pierre Daimpre was born late in 1884 in Sowton, Devon. His father Ysidore was a minister, later the vicar of Colebrooke in Devon, and Curate in the island of Alderney. In 1891, the family was living in Alderney, where Ysidore was then 50 years old, his wife Mary 38, and their inevitable half dozen minister's children ranged from Charles (15) through Alfred (13) and our Pierre, then six, to his delightfully-named sister Mezahab Wolf (4), younger brother Guy (2) and new-born Nora.

By 1901 Pierre's family was in Colebrooke, near Crediton, where his father was still clergyman and schoolmaster - and Marcel and Louis had

A nativity play in the 1930s

arrived. Our Daimpre drops out of the records for a while, but must have been educated and ordained. His parents came from Ireland, and it is possible that he went to Dublin, where both his parents were born, to attend Trinity College. In 1918, Pierre married Margery Conyers in Blandford Forum, Dorset. Four years later, they came to All Saints. There were Boxing Day dances and a Whist Drive held in the Wight school, as well as a Parish Tea and Social. Many shopkeepers would contribute, and an article in the *Harbury and Ladbroke News* of December 1982 recollects that Bob Thornicroft's shop would bake special long square-section sandwich loaves for the occasion. Pierre returned to Devon, in the 1933 telephone book for Newton Abbot. He died there in 1940.

The Reverend Capps in a biretta, with the choir. Tony Hodges is second from the left, and his elder brother, John, is behind him. John was called up in 1939; 'Alas, I have been without a server', wrote Mr Capps.

∽ 1930-1947 ∼
Alfred Frank Capps

ALFRED CAPPS is named 'Albert' on the record in church, but since the spelling there is sometimes erratic, I'm going to go with 'Alfred'. The Reverend Capps was an ex-army man and bachelor who had served in the Royal Artillery in the First World War, and he came to Harbury in 1930. He made several changes which were quite 'High Church'. They included incense carried in a 'boat' or censer and an Angelus bell, and establishing the Lady Chapel for smaller services. Boys from the school would go up to the church at midday to ring the Angelus.

Mr Capps put in the sanctuary or 'everlasting' red light over the chancel, and changed the cassocks and surplices on the choir and servers. The latter, and the carriers of the cross and candles (often Harold Webb and his twin brothers Don and John) had lace edges to their white surplices. They processed from the vestry behind the organ, which had formerly housed the children's corner; this and the font were moved to near the north door – which accommodated the growing numbers of children, especially for christenings. Reg Farrow, the Headmaster of the village school, was choirmaster.

There were also classes at the vicarage in useful skills – covering wooden stools with seagrass and edging trays with

Roland, John and Tony Hodges in surplices, 1934

The Christmas crib was first introduced by the Reverend Capps in 1931, and is in use to this day.

woven wickerwork. Mr Capps worked with the Royal British Legion to record the village losses in the Great War on a memorial plaque.

In 1931, he introduced the Christmas crib which is used to this day. A picture of him with the choir shows him in a biretta, a stiff hat more often worn by Roman Catholic clerics; and apparently a splendid

87

cope presented to him by Miss Hylda Nickalls, then resident in Pan's Gardens, caused quite a stir.

The Reverend Capps was much-liked in the village and sadly missed when he retired to clergy accommodation in Tettenhall in the West Midlands.

∾ 1947-1955 ∾
David A G Atcheson

DAVID ATCHESON and his family lived in the village from 1947, and are remembered for keeping chickens in the churchyard. The Reverend Atcheson used to push his children round the village in what was described as a disreputable old pram. He seems to have moved on to Studley, near Alcester, where he is fondly remembered. In 1996, at least one villager there regretted the closure of Mr Atcheson's garden. 'Lost to the village will be a parcel of the Vicarage garden, made available by its then incumbent, the late, and much-respected Rev David Atcheson. Seldom used in recent times, a bronze plaque, displayed at the entrance, and here copied below, explained all. Appreciated by many in its day, who has mourned its passing?'

ST. MARY'S GARDENS
THESE GARDENS WERE PROVIDED
BY THE GENEROSITY OF THE
PARISHIONERS OF STUDLEY AS A
PLACE OF REST AND QUIET FOR
ALL WHO MAY WISH TO USE THEM.
DEDICATED BY
THE RIGHT REV. C.K.N.BARDSLEY. C.B.E.,D.D.
LORD BISHOP OF COVENTRY
ON 24TH OCTOBER 1960.

∾ Tom ∾
and the Tom Hauley Room

AMUEL THOMAS Hauley was born in Leamington in 1907, and
came to Harbury from Wavendon in Buckinghamshire, where he
had moved as a boy, in 1932. Tom's father had a smallholding at
West End cottage in Mill Street, selling mostly eggs and poultry. Tom
arrived to find a church choir with six men and a number of boys. The
choirmaster of Wavendon recommended him for the choir, and Tom
joined the church choir on Ash Wednesday 1932, becoming a lifelong
stalwart, singing through the reigns of six vicars until his retirement
in October 1983. He was a longstanding member of the PCC, a school
'manager' or governor and a churchwarden. He mowed the churchyard
and raised and lowered the church flag on special days.

In 1939, he began winding the church clock, a daily task that he
continued all his life, excepting only holidays, illness and once, the
distraction of the church fete. He was a familiar figure, cycling, and
sometimes rowing along on his bike through the village wearing a tweed
cap or trilby. He was a good friend to Father Roy Mackley, the village's
bachelor vicar.

On his death on July 22nd, 1987, he bequeathed his cottage and garden
to the church and diocese, and these were sold to provide the funds for
the parish room named in his honour. Tom might have been surprised
at the extent of the room named in his memory; all he had asked was
that the church install a toilet.

THE TOM HAULEY ROOM

The most significant change to the church since Victorian times came
with the building of the Tom Hauley Room, part parish room, part
church hall. Its sliding wall makes it wonderfully flexible, and its kitchen
and toilets, including a disabled toilet, add to the church facilities. A
photograph of Tom with Mrs Sarah Enefer, widow of the village blacksmith, welcomes you to this valuable space.

Tom first made bequests to his friends and family in his will of July 1987, and then left the residue of his estate to the Parochial Church Council of All Saints and to the Diocesan Board of Finance, to be shared equally. 'for such general purposes as he said council and said board shall think fit'. The sale of his cottage and garden, and the building of two houses whose names – Bellringer and Hauley – financed two projects. The Diocese refurbished a room at the old diocesan offices in Palmeston Road, Coventry. It also was known as the Tom Hauley Room, but was lost when they moved offices some time ago to Hilltop, close to the Cathedral.

Tom Hauley and Mrs Sarah Enefer

All Saints' Parochial Church Council built the room that now extends from the north door of the church. The architects were Brown Langstone and Matthews of Warwick, whose Mr Grimwade dealt with the works. The tender, dated January 1988, was valued at £109,132.00. A contract was signed in March 1989 with Leam Castle, the local company headed by a parishioner, David Clarke, and construction commenced the following month. A small retrospective grant from Warwickshire County Council helped pay for the chairs.

Some graves were moved and gravestones resited after permission had been sought and granted by the families involved. Part of the boundary wall in Crown Street was demolished as access to the building site. The Osborne Memorial had to be moved from the rear of the church to its present position. The window to the left of the north door was filled with matching stone.

The contract was completed at the end of 1989 and the new room was dedicated by the then vicar, The Reverend Antony Rowe, on December 3rd, 1989. At the time of writing, there are plans to refurbish and update the toilets, and then the kitchen. External decoration is complete, and the interior will follow. The room is well used and is a huge asset to both the Church and the community.

∼ 1956-1983 ∼
Frederick Roy Mackley
Father Mac

ROY MACKLEY was the minister in Harbury from 1956 to 1983. He was a gentle, spiritual bachelor, content with silence and simplicity, who brought his natural peace to those in trouble or suffering loss - all of which contrasted with his uninhibited approach to amateur theatre.

Frederick Roy Mackley was born in Leicestershire, and was educated at Lutterworth Grammar School, where he became Head Boy. He studied at University College, Reading, gaining a first class honours degree in Philosophy from the University of London, and then a graduate Diploma in Education.

He became classics master at Bembridge Public School on the Isle of Wight. In 1927, he began theological training at the College of the

Father Roy Mackley

Demolition of the vicarage in Church Street

Resurrection in Mirfield, West Yorkshire. He was ordained priest in 1930 and appointed Assistant Curate of the Abbey Church of St Mary, Nuneaton. He was a popular man there, involving himself in the Church Union, the Society for the Propagation of the Gospel, and youth organisations like the Boy Scouts. In 1948, Roy became Vicar of All Saints' Church, Burton Dassett with Northend – the 'Cathedral of the Hills'. He was held in such esteem in Nuneaton that the Mayor and Corporation of the town turned out in their robes for his induction. During his service in Burton Dassett, the old church was cleaned for the first time in fifty years and the churchyard wall rebuilt.

In 1956, he moved to Harbury, living in the vicarage and cared for throughout his ministry by his faithful housekeeper, Beatrice Mary Mallabone. He developed his skills in engaging young people with very successful children's Lent services and with family services on the first Sunday of each month. He encouraged the 'Crusaders' children's church and saw its numbers rise throughout his ministry. He was an active and dedicated governor of the church school for many years.

Father Roy embraced evolution rather than revolution. In his time, the organ was restored and updated, and the bells were rehung. In December, 1979, a sound system was installed, and new lighting was dedicated and first used at the Family Eucharist on Advent Sunday, 30th November, 1980.

In May, 1974, the *Harbury News*, later the *Harbury and Ladbroke News*, was first published with the financial and moral support of the Church, a combination of All Saints' Parish Magazine and a local diary edited by Peter Phillips. It was instigated by Valentine Du Buisson, and forty years later is still thriving. At first published six times a year, it quickly became monthly. By 1979, it was judged the best parish magazine in the Diocese, and it went forward to the national final.

The March winds of 1979 brought down the churchyard's old chestnut tree, which had provided conkers for generations of village children. The remains were taken down as propping would be impractical and unsightly. A new chestnut tree was planted in its place. At Easter, 1982, the first Roman Catholic Mass was held in the church, replacing the Mass centre in the library at Harbury Hall. Methodist services followed, starting in December, 1982. The Christmas Carol Service in 1978 was the first to be held in candlelight, using candleholders made and installed by Peter Holt. The brass and ebony Processional Cross was Father Roy's property, left to the church on his retirement.

On the 25th August, 1985, Father Roy consecrated the Aumbry, to the right of the Lady Chapel, fulfilling a long-held ambition. This special cupboard, purchased with a gift from Miss Ethel Cook of Brentwood, contains reserved sacrament for use at any time.

Father Mac retained his love of music and reading. He enjoyed acting in Harbury Theatre Group productions, and was its honorary president for many years. Invited to play Squire Hardcastle in a production of *She Stoops to Conquer*, he modestly remarked that he had played the part before; sixty years before, as it turned out, as a schoolboy of 16. He arrived at the first rehearsal word-perfect, of course. In this role, as the Bishop of Lax in *See How They Run*, and as a retired colonel in *Black Comedy*, he revealed natural comic timing, and a broader mind and greater understanding of the modern world than many might have expected of him.

In April 1983, he retired from his ministry in Harbury. He had commented in February 1983 that he was 'very fit and healthy and fully active', but that he had continued twelve years beyond the age officially regarded as retirement for the clergy. His decision was based on his determination that Harbury would not have a vicar who was an invalid or was, in his words, 'getting beyond it'.

The former vicar of Southam, who preached at a service to celebrate Roy's 25 years in Harbury, wrote that he had an unwillingness to spend time on trivia – 'when he does say something, it's worth waiting for'. His great friend Tom Hauley said of him 'Behind that quiet unhurried manner lies a life devoted to his work. Harbury is a better place for his ministry among us'.

Roy retired to the College of St Barnabas in Lingfield, ('a good place to meet my Maker', he once remarked), where he continued his spiritual work both in the college and by taking services in local parishes right up to his death.

Asked once what he would say to God when he met Him face to face, Roy answered 'I shall say "Lord, have mercy on me, a sinner"'. This honourable man, after fifty years in the priesthood, had far less to confess than most.

The retired Canon Roy Churchill served the church though its interregnum until the appointment of Canon Rowe in August 1983.

∾ Beatrice Mary Mallabone ∾

MISS MALLABONE is deserving of an entry of her own in this church story. She was housekeeper to Father Roy Mackley from 1960 until his retirement in 1983, and a unique and unforgettable character.

Beatrice Mary Mallabone was born in Nuneaton on August 15th, 1898. Her mother died when she was a few days old, and she was brought up by a childless couple she called Aunt and Uncle. She was devoted to them, and cared for them until their deaths. She became apprenticed to a tailor, and became expert at tailoring. She was a regular worshipper and a Sunday School teacher at St Mary's Abbey Church, Nuneaton, and it was to the house she shared with her Aunt that Roy Mackley moved when he was bombed out of his house in the town.

In 1948, Roy moved to Burton Dassett, and Miss Mallabone joined him as his housekeeper, a role she continued throughout his years in Harbury. She was a familiar sight in the village in her battered hat, striding up the middle of Church Street as if the motor car had never been invented.

When Roy retired in May 1983, Miss Mallabone moved to the Limes retirement home in Stratford. The same month, she suffered a stroke, and died a little later in Stratford Hospital, her life's work done. She had served Father Roy, the village and her God loyally and faithfully.

∾ 1983 -1992 ∾
Canon Antony Rowe

THE JOINING of Harbury and Ladbroke was confirmed on August 1st, 1983. The collation of the first Rector of the United Benefice, Canon A S B Rowe was on September 23rd, 1983. That month, Tony Rowe, his wife Jean and their two sons, Stephen and Nicholas, moved into the newly redecorated vicarage. His daughter Anne was married and living and teaching in Coventry. He moved from the Coventry Parish of St Mary Magdalen, Chapelfields, taking over from both Roy Mackley in Harbury and Canon Fishley in Ladbroke, and combining the two parishes in his care. Roy Mackley wrote

Canon Anthony Rowe

to welcome him to 'one of the friendliest places in the whole country'. Stephen, who was 24 when the family moved to Harbury, went on to be ordained himself. Father Antony was a Canon, a title bestowed on clergy with a record of honourable service in a Diocese.

Antony Rowe was born in Stoke, Coventry, on March 29th, 1926, the only child of Oscar and Marjorie Rowe. He attended King Henry VIll Grammar School, and then was called up to serve in the army from August, 1944 for four years – two of them in India. He became a primary school teacher in Coventry and then attended St John's College,

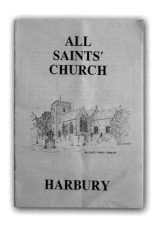

ALL
SAINTS'
CHURCH

HARBURY

*Jean Rowe's history
of the church*

Durham, to prepare for ordination. He met his future wife, Jean, at a youth club at St John's, Coventry and they married at that church on April 15th 1952.

He was ordained priest in September, 1956, became curate at St Luke's Church, Holbrooks and then Vicar of St Mary Magdalene.

From 1983 to 1992 he was rector of Harbury and Ladbroke. His churchwardens said of his nine years in Harbury, 'his dedication to Our Lord is absolute, and because of that his ministry to the people of Harbury and Ladbroke has been of a very high order. Whether churchgoers or not, all were precious in his sight'. They in turn 'relished his sense of fun' and his memorable slips of the tongue.

On retirement, he and Jean reluctantly left Harbury and went to live in Mickleton in Gloucestershire. In his touching words 'it is an unwritten rule that a rector or vicar leaves a parish clear for his successor. It is not so unwise and possibly in the long run makes good sense'. He added 'we shall think of you often and with great love and affection'. Father Antony continued an active ministry, celebrating the 40th anniversary of his ordination in September, 1996 and the 50th at St James, Marston Sicca, in 2006.

During the interregnum, the Church was fortunate to be able to call on the services of two retired ministers living in Harbury, Canon Roy

Churchill and Father Peter Snow.

Just before Father Antony's retirement, in October, 1992, the church boiler, once lovingly tended by Harry Windsor, was replaced at a cost of ten thousand pounds. It had sulked ever since Harry's retirement as boiler engineer. Charles Catt took over as 'master of the timers and thermostats'.

∾ 1993-2007 ∾
Canon Philip Roy Brown

IT WAS Father Roy's idea to reshape the chancel, introducing a nave altar closer to the congregation, and having new altar rails made by local craftsmen using wood from the old pews. He encouraged the involvement of lay people in the work previously done only by ordained clergy, and in the year 2000, he instigated Harvest in Harbury, celebrating the many talents of the village. His thirteen and a half years in Harbury, in his own words, 'flew by'.

Philip Roy Brown is a Birmingham man, born in Hall Green in November, 1941, and a student at Moseley Grammar School. He enjoyed all sports, especially rugby, tennis and badminton. His family moved to Small Heath where his mother ran a general store, and Roy became a cost accountant, and later a Fellow of the Institute of Administrative Accountants, working at Joseph Lucas and later at GKN – Guest, Keen and Nettlefold.

Canon Philip Roy Brown

In 1956, he met Pam, then a nurse, at St Oswald's Church in Small Heath, and they married in 1962, moving to Shirley. Roy became church-warden at St Oswald's, and they both continued their involvement long after they had moved away. Claire, Helen and David were born between 1964 and 1970. Pam later became a Hospital Social Worker. Roy maintained his interests in sport, music and theatre, and became a member of the City of Birmingham Symphony Orchestra chorus. He and Pam

later made significant contributions to the music in Harbury church, Pam developing the choir, and son David and his wife returning to sing at many events. He remarked of his musical family, on his appointment to Harbury, 'We all sing!'

Roy had been confirmed in his faith at the age of twelve, and so began a lifetime of regular worship. In 1977, his life changed direction. He was accepted to train for the ministry – a friend remarking that he didn't know why Roy had left it so long. From 1978 to 1980 he was a student at St Stephen's House Theological College in Oxford, meeting the family at weekends in Oxford, and sometimes travelling home to Birmingham on a motorcycle. Then he became

Jeff Bedford and Father Roy during the building of the new dais, designed by Neville Ellis

curate to Emmanuel Church, Highters Heath. In 1981 he was ordained priest, and in 1983 he became priest in charge at St Mark's in Washwood Heath. In 1987, he moved to become the vicar of Tysoe, Oxhill and Whatcote, and from there to Harbury as Rector in 1993. He came to Harbury, in his own words. 'because it felt right'. Roy became Rural Dean of the Southam area in 1996.During Roy's incumbency, the ROC (Roof, Organ and Clock) fund completed its repairs and improvements; the family service became a main service with lay involvement and the Jubilate music group; the Talk it Through discussion group started; and Alpha Courses and the First Light services began. Roy appointed Pastoral Assistants, and strengthened the Church's links with the village school. Since his Ordination, Roy always regarded Church people as family, having learned from another priest that a belief in the family of the Church has the power to transform.

Roy was made Canon in recognition of his pastoral work and contribution to rural ministry. His whole attitude to ministry is that he saw himself as the servant of all, making it clear that he was available to anyone, twenty-four hours a day, seven days a week. Roy always tried to take part in the whole life of the village; to go wherever he was invited; to meet the people where they were. The strength of the village's affection for him was demonstrated at the farewell events that marked his retirement to Kenilworth in March 2007, which included a very special *This is Your Life*, to which so many groups and individuals contributed.

∼ 2008 ∼
The Reverend Craig Groocock

REVEREND CRAIG was born in Market Drayton, Shropshire, on the 4th of April 1965 to what he describes as 'a very ordinary, working class couple in a very ordinary home', the younger of two brothers (Chris was born in 1959, and is also an ordained minister). Craig records that he was born on the day that John Lennon wrote the song 'Help!'

He was baptised at three months, and had no church upbringing and no early experience of the church. But at the age of 15, he was taken along to the local church youth club by his older brother and became involved in the large servers' team at St Mary's, Market Drayton. The

Jessica, Craig, Su and Elliot at the renewal of Su and Craig's
Wedding vows, August 2012

Christian faith became increasingly important to him and he was confirmed in 1980. It was at this point that he met Su McClellan and they
started going out together. They married at St Mary's in 1987. There
was no family expectation that Craig would stay on at school. So he left
at 17 and began work as an apprentice printer. However, both he and
Su felt called to full time ministry, and following their marriage, they
began training with the Church Army in Blackheath, London. Craig
was commissioned, along with Su, as a Church Army Captain in 1990.

His first post was as Project Worker for the Shrewsbury Churches'
Youth Project. Following this he was appointed youth and children's
minister for two churches in Bedworth, Warwickshire. The family moved
to Warwick in 1996 where Craig became youth minister in the Warwick
team and leader of the Warwick youth project. In 2000 the Bishop of
Coventry appointed Craig as his Diocesan youth advisor. During this
time he felt a calling to the ordained ministry and explored this with
the diocese at great length. He was accepted for ordination preparation
and began training at Queen's College, Birmingham, in 2003.

Craig was ordained in 2005 and served his curacy at St Nicholas Church, Kenilworth. He was appointed to Harbury and Ladbroke in May 2008. Su and Craig described Harbury and Ladbroke as 'their perfect parish', and they have thrown themselves, heart and soul, into village life. Craig has led the church through growth and evolution, taking the whole congregation with him. He has introduced a new pattern of evening services, embracing innovations including Celtic Christianity alongside the traditional prayer book. In his time, the church has been completely refloored under the watchful eye of Jeff Bedford. Under Craig's supervision, Annie Goldthorp has served her curacy with us, contributing enormously to both village and Church life, and becoming ordained in 2012. Since 2011 Craig has served as Rural Dean for Southam Deanery.

Su remains a church army officer and has worked full time in youth work and with young parents since her commissioning. She is currently the Midlands manager for the Bible*lands* charity, recently renamed *Embrace the Middle East*. Their two children are Jessica (born in 1992), currently at Durham University reading Politics, and Elliot (born in 1997) at Warwick School. Craig is a black belt in the martial arts sport Shotokan Karate. He enjoys amateur astronomy, keeping fit and playing the Ukulele, He founded the Harbury Ukulele Group – HUG or the HUGGERS – in the village.

The church has become a venue for music, theatre and art exhibitions

∾ Ann Goldthorp ∾
Curate and Priest 2011

ANNIE was born in Cheltenham in 1959 and was adopted as a baby. She grew up with her older brother and they lived with a loving family in Olton, Solihull. She attended an all girls grammar school and when she left, she wanted to be earning and learning at the same time. She secured an apprenticeship at Land Rover, in what was then known as the Personnel Department. In fact she made history – she was the first female apprentice Land Rover had ever employed. She enjoyed every minute of it – the greater the challenge, the happier she was. She left there in 1986 having had a wonderful time. She married in 1983, but unfortunately it was not to be a lasting one, and they parted in 1992. Jeremy was born in 1987 when they were living in Hull, and he lived with her until he moved London to do his degree in film studies. They came to Warwick in 1998, and Annie very quickly got involved with youth activities at both St Nicholas' and St Mary's – briefly under the direction of Craig Groocock, who was then Youth Officer. Craig led the preparation classes when Jeremy was confirmed!

Reverend Annie Goldthorpe, 2012

Annie had been working for a magazine publisher for ten years, and then in 2004, she had her own design magazine. It was around the same time that thoughts of ordination were beginning, with 'nudges' from various members of the clergy, and by 2007 she started the vocations process. She was recommended for a Bishop's panel the following year, and started training in the autumn of 2008. She has found it tough working full time and training over three years. Annie was appointed Curate to Harbury and Ladbroke in 2011, and found Easter in the villages to be a deeply spiritual time. She had the added bonus of being Deacon at the Chrism Eucharist on Maundy Thursday at the Cathedral – a rare privilege. Annie says she is not an academic and writing essays and lengthy pieces of theological reflection does not come easily to her. However, when she looks back, she can see that she has grown spiritually, become far more confident and developed a much more reflective approach to ministry. In July 2011 she was ordained Deacon at Coventry Cathedral, and ordained priest the following year.

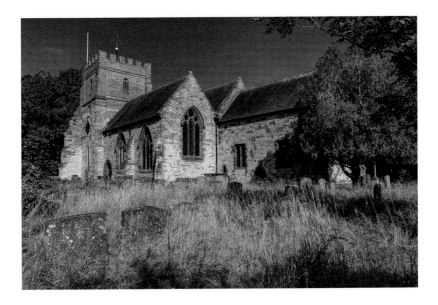

With the ordination of the first woman priest at All Saints' Church Harbury, the Church moves faithfully and confidently into the new millennium.

∽ Further reading ∽

Articles in the *Harbury and Ladbroke News* by Celia Barrett, Charles Keeling, Linda Ridgeley, Mary Thompson and the Reverend Roy Mackley.

Hungry Harbury, a guide to a Warwickshire village. Published by the Harbury Society. Linda Ridgeley, Hon Secretary, December 1980.

All Saints' Church, Harbury, Tower. Notes about the church tower and bells, by Neville Ellis, June 2000.

All Saints' Church, Harbury, by Jean Rowe, undated.

The History of All Saint's Church, Harbury, Warwickshire by the Reverend F R Mackley, Vicar, 1956-83.

The History of Chesterton and Kingston, by Dorothy A Noden, 1978. New edition, 1988.

Welcome to Chesterton Church, a short history and guide. Anonymous.

The Buildings of England: Warwickshire, by Nikolaus Pevsner and Alexandra Wedgwood, Penguin Books, First printed 1966.

Faith, Pride and Works: Medieval Church Building, by Tom McNeill, Tempus Publishing Ltd, 2006.

The Parish Churches of Medieval England, by Colin Platt, Chancellor Press, 1981.

How to Read a Church, by Richard Taylor, Rider Publishing, 2003.

The Antiquities of Warwickshire, by Sir William Dugdale, 1730.

A History of the County of Warwick, 1945.

Pigot and Co's Commercial Directory.

Kelly's Trade Directory.

Henry Beighton's Map of Warwickshire, 1728.

The Spire, by William Golding, Faber and Faber, 1964.

A collection of documents, photographs and films of the village
is housed in a converted classroom at the village
primary school.

Harbury Heritage Centre is accessible to the public on certain days
outside school time so the collection can be used and appreciated
by a larger audience.

Harbury Heritage Centre is housed at
Harbury C.E. Primary School, Mill Street, Harbury,
Leamington Spa, Warwickshire CV33 9HR
For further details of opening times and events, contact:
nigel.chapman@hotmail.co.uk

Harbury Heritage is self-funding. Donations are welcome.

The Centre is managed and run by volunteers. If you are interested
in joining the group, please contact them at the address above.
The Centre would welcome items which could be added
to the collection.